FRIDA KAHLO SELF-PORTRAIT WITH CROPPED HAIR

JODI ROBERTS

THE MUSEUM OF MODERN ART, NEW YORK

***SELF-PORTRAIT WITH CROPPED HAIR*, BY THE MEXICAN ARTIST FRIDA KAHLO,** counters what we have come to expect from her work. In place of the bright palette that enlivens many of her paintings, it is rendered almost entirely in neutral hues of brown, black, beige, and dusty pink. Her hallmark clothing—colorful shirts and skirts inspired by indigenous Mexican dress—has been exchanged for a dark, ill-fitting men's suit. Her long hair—often shown braided, piled atop her head, and laced with ribbons **[FIG. 1]**—is here reduced to a short, slicked-back crop. The monkeys, dogs, and other intriguing creatures that often populate her paintings have been replaced with long strands of hair that seem to wiggle on the floor and up the rungs of the chair with a life of their own. Where Kahlo's paintings often include inscriptions describing their subject matter and date of completion, *Self-Portrait with Cropped Hair* features lyrics from a song popular at the time it was made: "Mira que si te quise, fué por el pelo, ahora que estás pelona, ya no te quiero" (Look, if I loved you it was for your hair. Now that you're without it I no longer love you).

Yet the work is unmistakably Kahlo's, not least for the face that stares resolutely at us from its surface. Kahlo's physiognomy is iconic: dark, piercing eyes crowned by full brows that meet in the middle; a short, slightly round nose; pert lips topped with a shadow of fuzz. The ready recognizability of the artist is due first and foremost to the dozens of self-portraits she made over the course of her career, but pictures of her made by others have also played a role. The camera, in particular, has been one of the principal ways in which her image has been disseminated. Her father photographed her during her younger years **[FIG. 2]**; later, she sat for celebrated modernists, including Edward Weston, Lola

Frida Kahlo (Mexican, 1907–1954). *Self-Portrait with Cropped Hair*. 1940. Oil on canvas, 15 ¾ x 11" (40 x 27.9 cm). THE MUSEUM OF MODERN ART, NEW YORK. GIFT OF EDGAR KAUFMANN, JR.

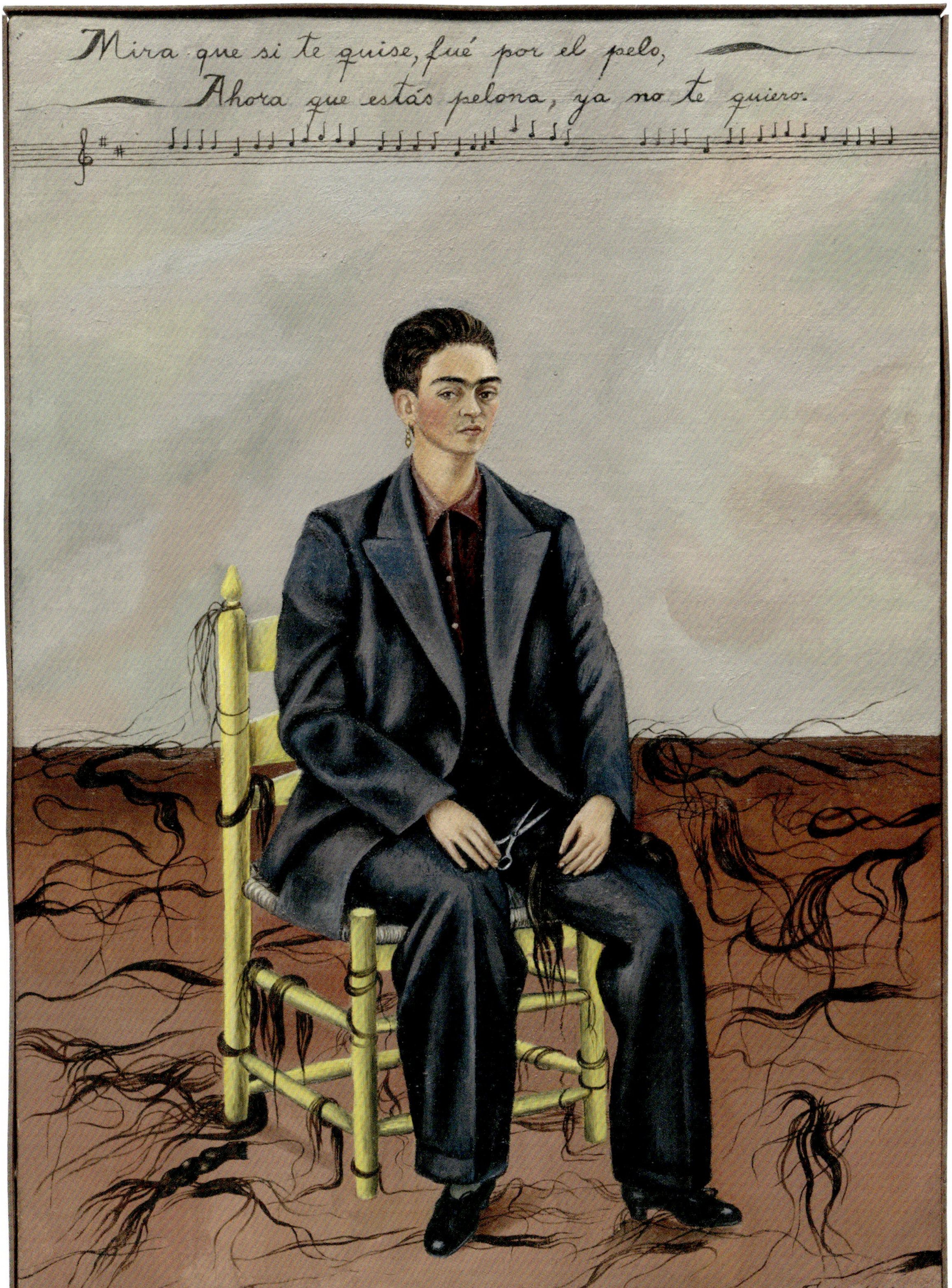
Mira que si te quise, fué por el pelo,
Ahora que estás pelona, ya no te quiero.
1940. Frida Kahlo.

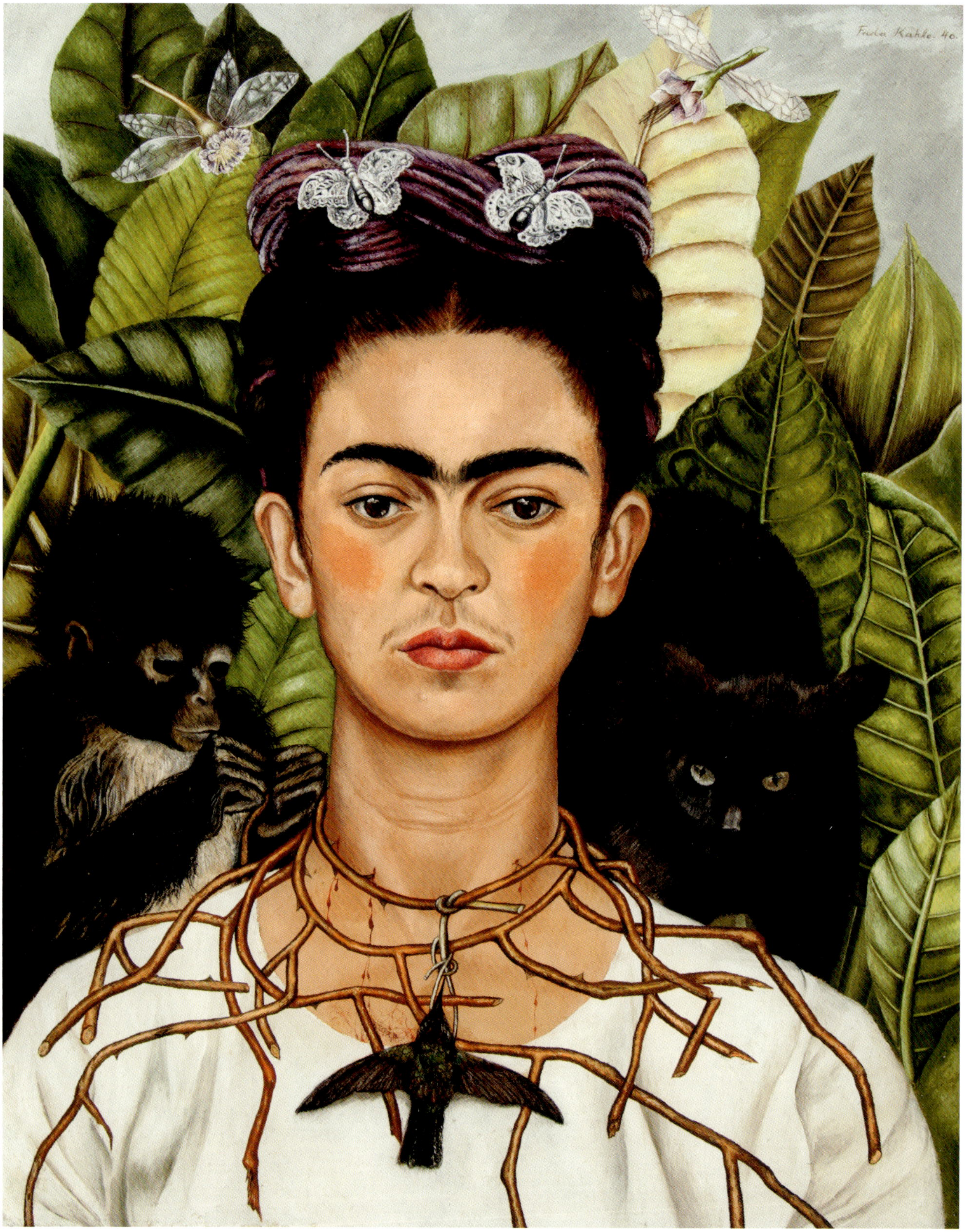
Frida Kahlo. 40.

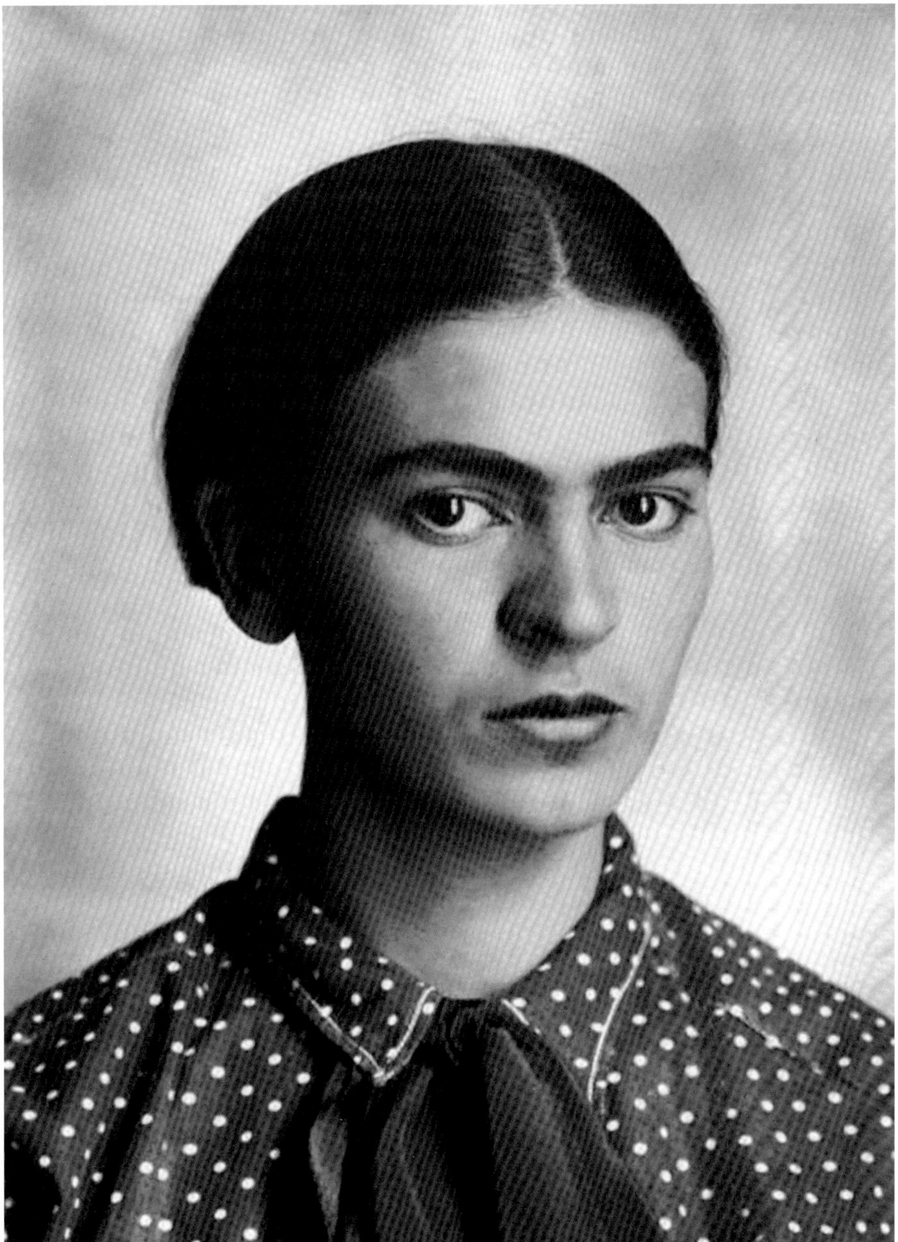

OPPOSITE: FIG. 1. Frida Kahlo (Mexican, 1907–1954). *Self-Portrait with Thorn Necklace and Hummingbird.* 1940. Oil on canvas, 24 1/16 x 18 1/2" (61.3 x 47 cm). HARRY RANSOM CENTER, THE UNIVERSITY OF TEXAS AT AUSTIN

ABOVE: FIG. 2. Photograph of Frida Kahlo by her father, Guillermo Kahlo, c. 1926. FRIDA KAHLO & DIEGO RIVERA ARCHIVE, MEXICO CITY

Álvarez Bravo, and Imogen Cunningham **[FIG. 3]**. She caught the eye of photojournalists and appeared in newspapers across Mexico and the United States. Since her death, in 1954, the myriad images of Kahlo created during her lifetime have been printed and reprinted en masse, feeding a phenomenon (known as "Fridamania") and a cultural industry that has produced a dizzying array of Kahlo-themed commodities.

Kahlo is celebrated as a master painter, but her personality and biography have also captured the imagination of millions of people. In no small part, this widespread love stems from the confessional nature of her work. Her self-portraiture, the genre she favored above all others, seems to divulge the subjective experience of an artist keenly attuned to her deepest psychological urges and core emotional truths. Kahlo insisted that her paintings flowed from an interior source: "My work consisted of eliminating everything that did not come from the internal lyrical motives that impelled me to paint," she explained in 1940, the year she made *Self-Portrait with Cropped Hair.* "Since my subject [has] always been my sensations, my states of mind and the profound reactions that life has been producing in me, I have frequently objectified all this in figures of myself."[1] The people closest to the artist have confirmed that an urgent exploration of her inner workings formed the basis of her creative activity. As her husband, the painter Diego Rivera, explained, "Frida is the only example in the history of art of an artist who tore open her chest and heart to reveal the biological truth of her feelings."[2] Kahlo's willingness to render her most private sentiments with unflinching candor transformed her into a symbol of personal integrity.

The "sensations" and "states of mind" that inspired *Self-Portrait with Cropped Hair* were no doubt acutely painful. Kahlo made the work in the wake of her (short-lived) divorce from Rivera in 1939. After a volatile decade of marriage, their relationship had become untenable. But the work is much more than the lament of a hurt lover. Like so many works by Kahlo, *Self-Portrait with Cropped Hair* reveals the artist's remarkable ability to disclose her most private emotional states by drawing upon a trove of social signifiers with origins in the exterior world. Although Kahlo is invoked today as a patron saint by those seeking profound self-knowledge and uncompromising self-expression, her paintings betray a willingness to adopt and discard at will varied—and sometimes contradictory—modes of self-expression. With strategies that, in hindsight, seem extraordinarily prescient in their attempts to navigate the vagaries of

FIG. 3. Imogen Cunningham (American, 1883–1976). *Frida Rivera*. 1931. Gelatin silver print, 8 ¼ x 6 ⅛" (21 x 15.6 cm). THE MUSEUM OF MODERN ART, NEW YORK. GIFT OF ALBERT M. BENDER

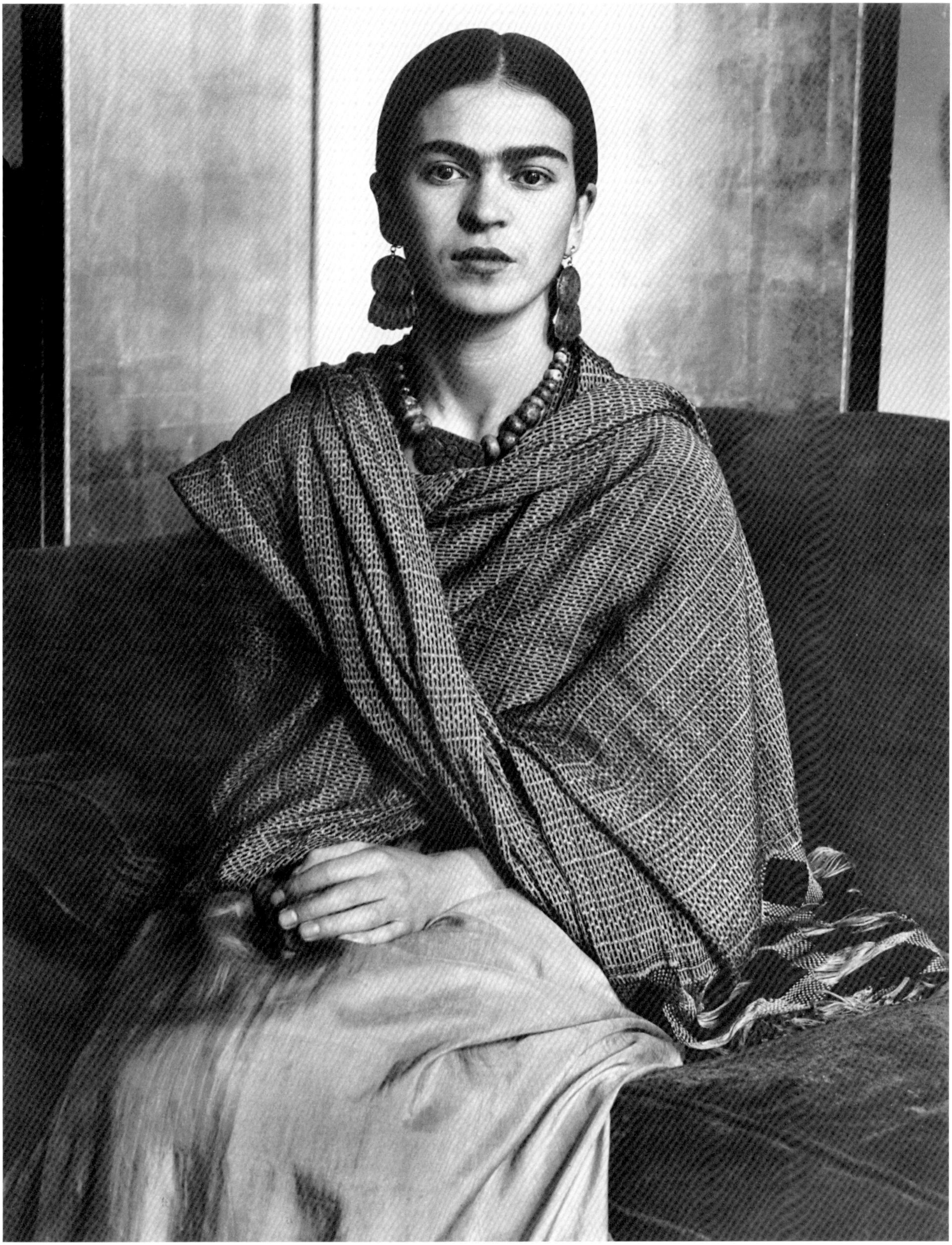

personal versus public identity, Kahlo's paintings cast doubt on the notion of a singular, stabile subjectivity, even as they seem to offer insights into the essential being of their maker. For all the ways it conforms to—and, more important, defies—our expectations of Kahlo's work, *Self-Portrait with Cropped Hair* reveals the artist to be a master of self-construction.[3]

Kahlo's oeuvre is often described as an autobiography in paint. Like all good autobiographers, Kahlo carefully picked and chose among facts and experiences when composing it. She emphasized details she considered foundational, including episodes that predate a fully formed, adult consciousness. She spent large parts of her life in her family home in Coyoacán, at the time a quiet residential neighborhood at the edge of Mexico City. Her mother, Matilde Calderón y González, came from Oaxaca and claimed both Spanish and indigenous blood. Guillermo Kahlo, her father, emigrated from Germany as a young man. The diversity of Kahlo's familial heritage provided rich ground for the artist's ingenious self-creation. *My Grandparents, My Parents, and I (Family Tree)* **[FIG. 4]** diagrams the cultural traditions Kahlo called her own: on the left, portraits of her mother and maternal grandparents float above a hilly landscape and flora native to Mexico; on the right, her father and paternal grandparents hover over a coastline that alludes to the Atlantic Ocean and to Europe beyond. At the center, Kahlo appears at three different stages of her early life—at conception, as a fetus, and as a small child. A red ribbon ties the young girl to her predecessors and their various cultural terrains.

Kahlo considered herself a child of the Mexican Revolution, the decade-long war that began in 1910 and resulted in the deaths of more than a million Mexican citizens.[4] The conflict erupted during the crisis of succession at the end of the authoritarian administration of Porfirio Díaz, who had ruled Mexico for three and a half decades. The ensuing bloody battles over the enfranchisement of the lower classes and agrarian peasantry transformed the nation's politics and economics as well as its heterogeneous cultural sphere. Díaz and his sympathizers preferred European cultural trends and erudite academic traditions that were far removed from the native arts of Mexico, a tendency in keeping with their favoring of foreign powers and upper-class Mexicans with interests overseas. But by the last decades of the nineteenth century, a fervent interest in indigenous history and culture emerged among Mexican intellectuals, artists, and writers. This search for manifestations of an authentic *mexicanidad* spawned a range of artistic responses, from heroic portrayals of the country's pre-Columbian past to modernist renderings of its indigenous present, as well as nourishing interest in folk art made and consumed by Mexico's masses.

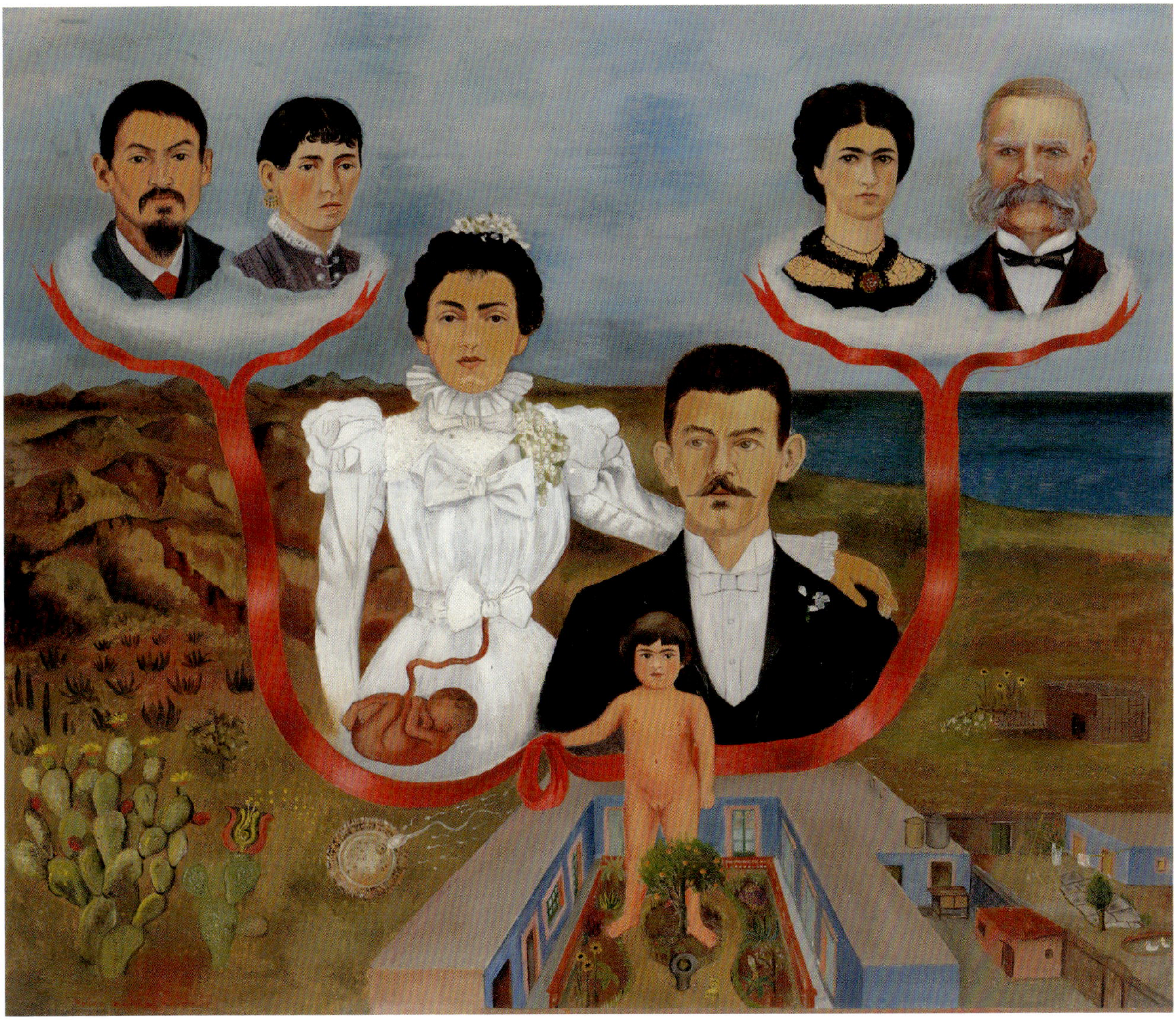

FIG. 4. Frida Kahlo (Mexican, 1907–1954). *My Grandparents, My Parents, and I (Family Tree)*. 1936. Oil and tempera on zinc, 12 ⅛ x 13 ⅝" (30.7 x 34.5 cm). THE MUSEUM OF MODERN ART, NEW YORK. GIFT OF ALLAN ROOS, M. D., AND B. MATHIEU ROOS

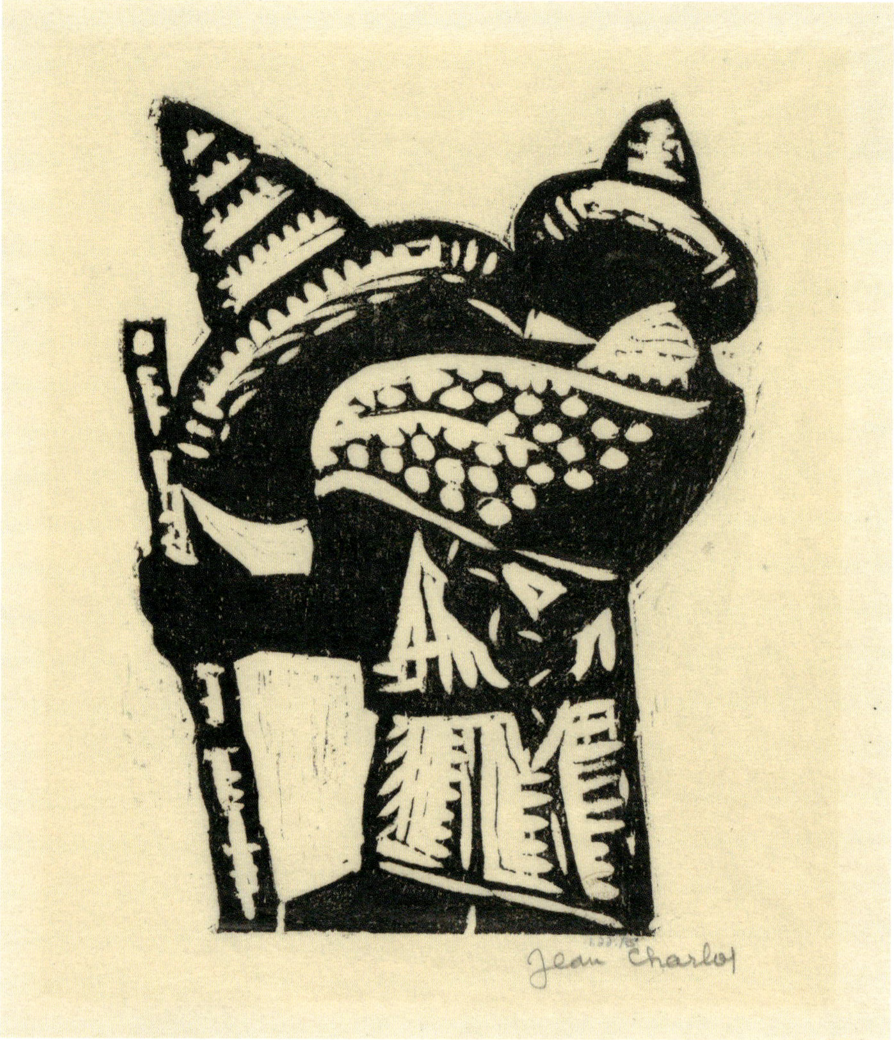

FIG. 5. Jean Charlot (French, 1898–1979). *Woman with a Child on Her Back*. 1924. Woodcut, 11 x 8 9/16" (28 x 21.7 cm). Artist's proof. THE METROPOLITAN MUSEUM OF ART, NEW YORK. THE HARRIS BRISBANE DICK FUND

The foundation of a new government in 1920 fueled these efforts to establish a Mexican culture that would account for the nation's multifaceted ethnic makeup and complex history while also embracing modernity in its varied social and cultural forms. Visual artists put their minds to creating new works that would strike a balance between the old and the new, the indigenous and the cosmopolitan. Jean Charlot [**FIG. 5**], a French transplant to Mexico, for example,

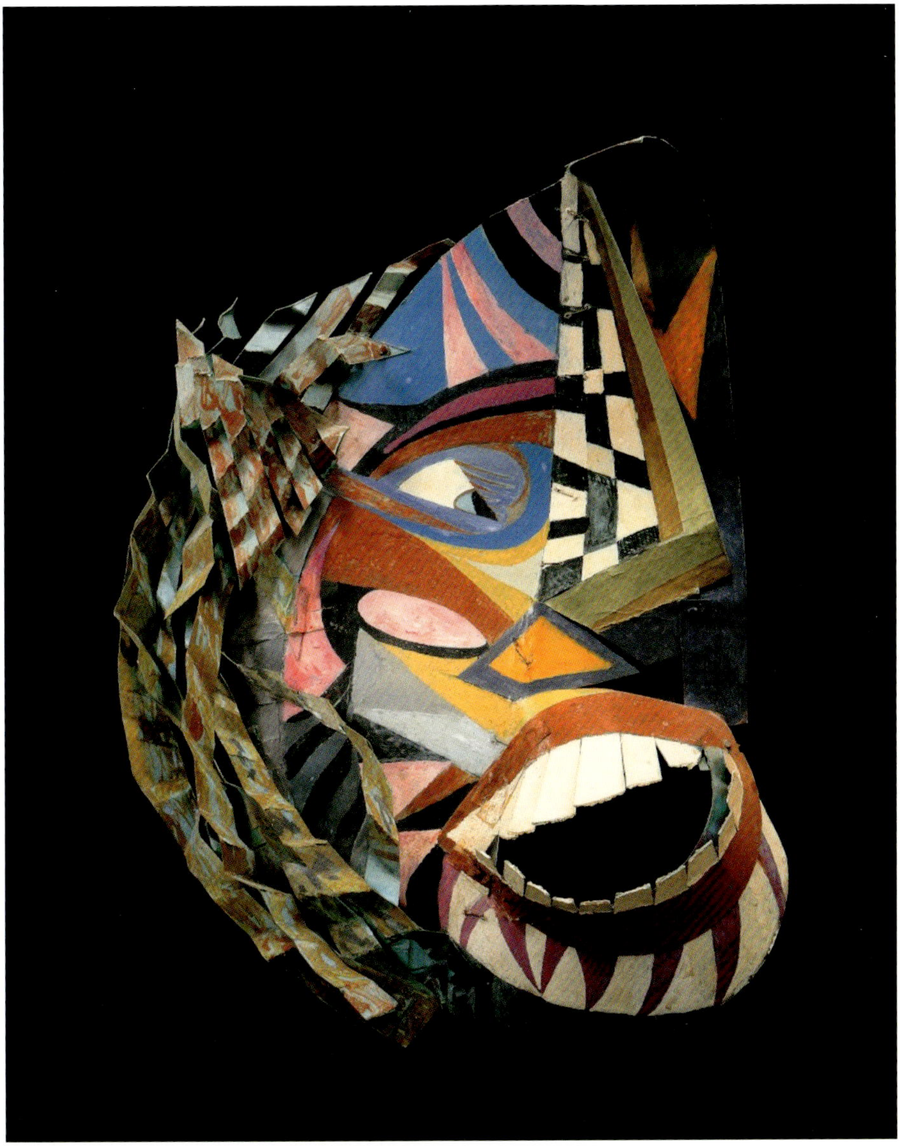

FIG. 6. Germán Cueto (Mexican, 1893–1975). *Mask I*. 1924. Paint on cardboard, 16 15⁄16 x 9 1⁄4 x 7 3⁄8" (43 x 23.5 x 18.5 cm). COLLECIÓN ANDRÉS BLAISTEN, MEXICO

offered a sympathetic view of Mexico's peasantry in woodblock prints, a medium appreciated by modernists for the directness of its process and the force of its visual effects. Germán Cueto paid homage to Mexico's folk arts with masks [**FIG. 6**] that simultaneously allude to indigenous costumes and contemporary art movements such as Cubism. In *Maya Women* (1926; **FIG. 7**), Roberto Montenegro rendered his subjects heroic by simplifying the curves of their

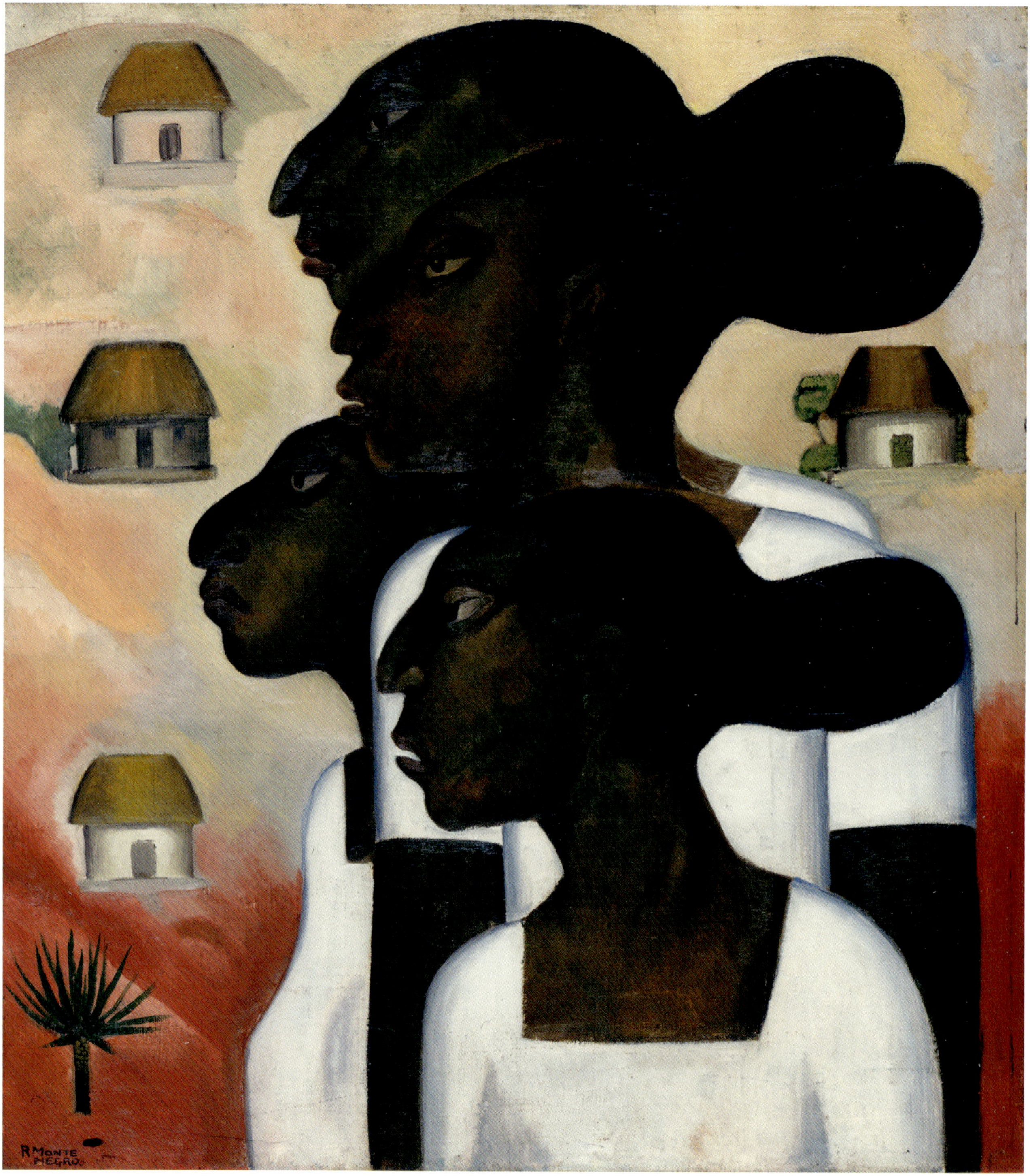
R MONTE
NEGRO

profiles into geometric forms; in defiance of academic tradition, he eschewed linear perspective, instead stacking his figures, one right behind another, in front of a horizonless, curtainlike landscape.

Kahlo was still young during the cultural efflorescence that followed the revolution, but she was exposed to the work of the period's leading artists. She saw Diego Rivera's monumental murals go up on the walls of the Secretaría de Educación Pública (SEP), the new ministry of education in Mexico City, with images and scenes that proclaimed Mexico's postrevolutionary ideals. As the most prolific muralist on the government's payroll, Rivera played a critical role in focusing the nation's attention on indigenous peoples, customs, and art forms. His frescos in the SEP (1923–28) covered tens of thousands of square feet with images of regional occupations and landscapes, popular religious festivals, and political celebrations. In a cycle of images in the SEP's Patio de las Fiestas (Courtyard of fiestas) known as *Corrido de la revolución* (Ballad of the revolution) (1928; **FIG. 8**), a ribbon inscribed with the lyrics of *corridos*, popular songs of the revolutionary era, ties one scene to the next. It is likely that Rivera took his cue for the use of such songs from José Guadalupe Posada, a printmaker who published popular songs on broadsides, and whose work was enjoying an enthusiastic revival in the postrevolutionary years. **[FIG. 9]**

Kahlo's reference to a popular song in *Self-Portrait with Cropped Hair* builds on this tradition of pairing musical and visual art forms and attests to her own deep investment in Mexican popular culture. Yet Kahlo's tune inverts the terms laid out by Posada and Rivera. Rather than demanding recognition for folk customs by projecting them onto walls and reproducing them in a medium intended for mass distribution, Kahlo brings the song—something shared by a broad audience—into the private realm. While well aware of the public art campaigns of her older peers, Kahlo matured at a moment when bombastic images trumpeting the value of indigenous and folk traditions began to be questioned by a younger generation of artists, and when the work of celebrity-seeking artists such as Rivera was criticized as overly propagandistic. Kahlo's paintings of the late 1930s and early 1940s, by contrast, are singular compositions, often intimate in scale and intended for private consumption. Her works suggest that true advocacy of Mexican culture requires a more thorough ingestion of popular traditions—a willingness to try them out as viable appendages to one's self.

FIG. 7. Roberto Montenegro (Mexican, 1885–1968). *Maya Women*. 1926. Oil on canvas, 31 ½ x 27 ½" (80 x 69.8 cm). THE MUSEUM OF MODERN ART, NEW YORK. GIFT OF NELSON A. ROCKEFELLER

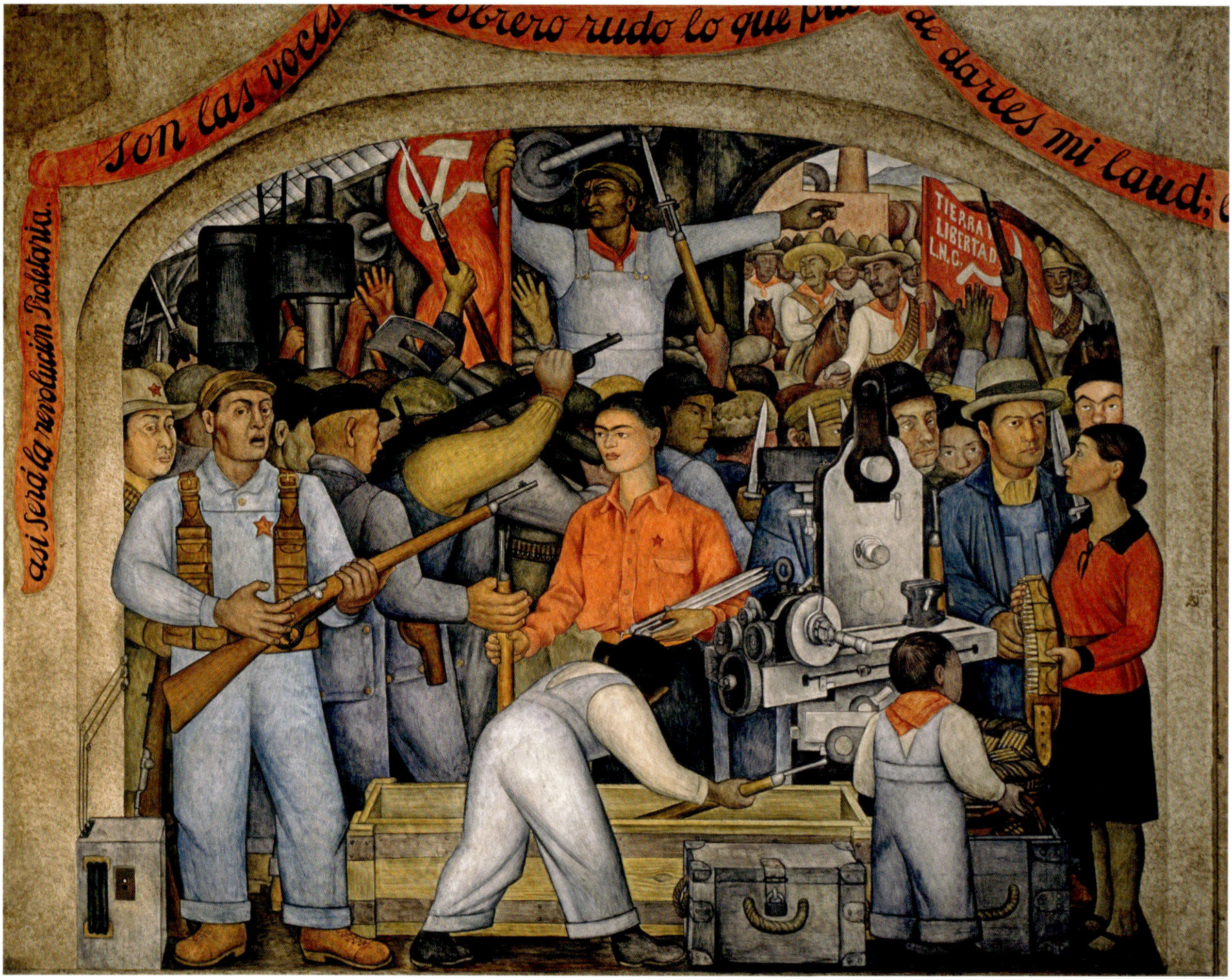

FIG. 8. Diego Rivera (Mexican, 1886–1957). *In the Arsenal*. 1928. Fresco, approx. 6' 7 7⁄8" x 13' 6" (203 x 398 cm).
PATIO DE LAS FIESTAS, SECRETARÍA DE EDUCACIÓN PÚBLICA, MEXICO CITY

To metabolize the lessons of indigenous art and popular culture, Kahlo kept examples of such work close at hand, in an enormous collection of pre-Columbian objects and Mexican folk art that she and Rivera amassed. References to art forms that predate Mexico's colonization regularly appear in her work **[FIG. 10]**, but she paid special attention to retablos (small devotional

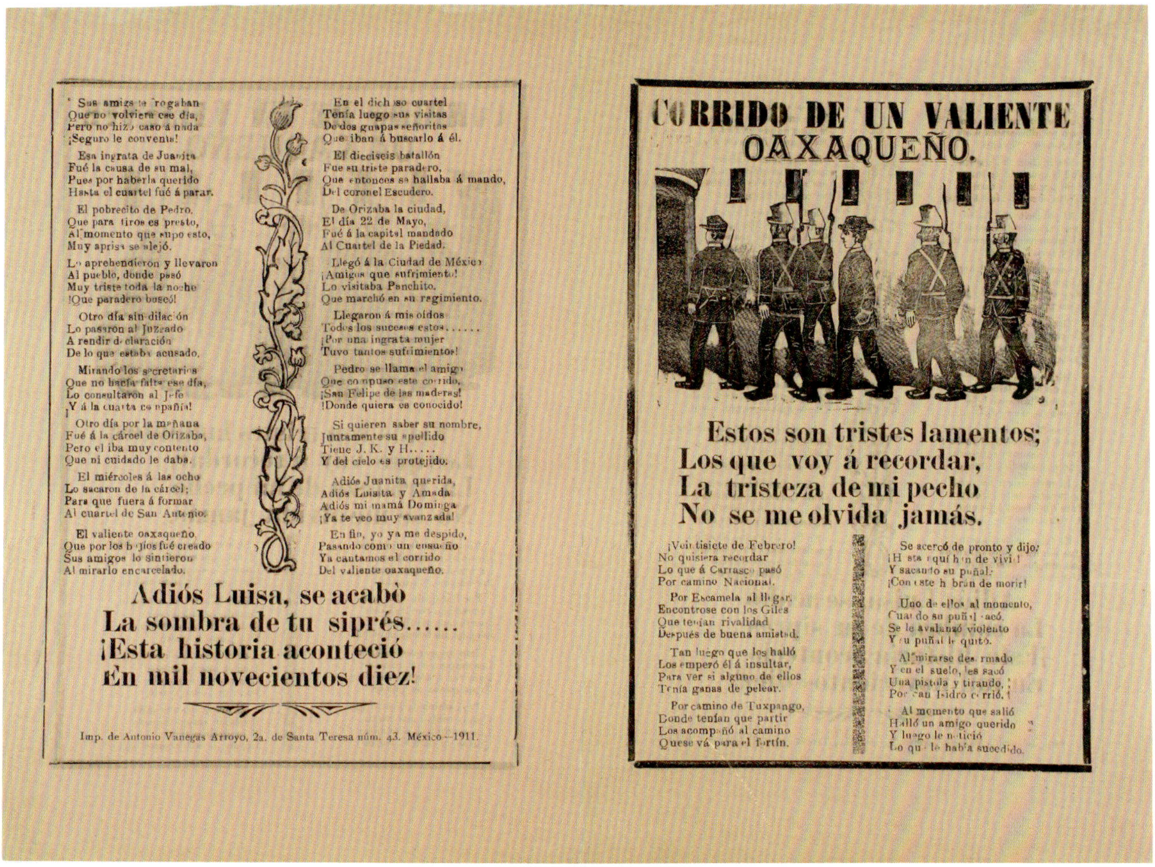

CORRIDO DE UN VALIENTE OAXAQUEÑO.

Estos son tristes lamentos;
Los que voy á recordar,
La tristeza de mi pecho
No se me olvida jamás.

¡Veintisiete de Febrero!
No quisiera recordar
Lo que á Carrasco pasó
Por camino Nacional.

Por Escamela al llegar,
Encontrose con los Giles
Que tenían rivalidad
Después de buena amistad.

Tan luego que los halló
Los empezó él á insultar,
Para ver si alguno de ellos
Tenía ganas de pelear.

Por camino de Tuxpango,
Donde tenían que partir
Los acompañó al camino
Quese vá para el fortín.

Se acercó de pronto y dijo:
¡Hasta aquí han de vivir!
Y sacando su puñal:
¡Con éste habrán de morir!

Uno de ellos al momento,
Cuando su puñal sacó,
Se le avalanzó violento
Y su puñal le quitó.

Al mirarse desarmado
Y en el suelo, les sacó
Una pistola y tirando,
Por San Isidro corrió.

Al momento que salió
Halló un amigo querido
Y luego le notició
Lo que le había sucedido.

Sus amigos le rogaban
Que no volviera ese día,
Pero no hizo caso á nada
¡Seguro le convenía!

Esa ingrata de Juanita
Fué la causa de su mal,
Pues por haberla querido
Hasta el cuartel fué á parar.

El pobrecito de Pedro,
Que para tiros es presto,
Al momento que supo esto,
Muy aprisa se alejó.

Lo aprehendieron y llevaron
Al pueblo, donde pasó
Muy triste toda la noche
¡Que paradero buscó!

Otro día sin dilación
Lo pasaron al Juzgado
A rendir declaración
De lo que estaba acusado.

Mirando los secretarios
Que no hacía falta ese día,
Lo consultaron al Jefe
¡Y á la cuarta compañía!

Otro día por la mañana
Fué á la cárcel de Orizaba,
Pero el iba muy contento
Que ni cuidado le daba.

El miércoles á las ocho
Lo sacaron de la cárcel;
Para que fuera á formar
Al cuartel de San Antonio.

El valiente oaxaqueño,
Que por los bajíos fué creado
Sus amigos lo sintieron
Al mirarlo encarcelado.

En el dichoso cuartel
Tenía luego sus visitas
De dos guapas señoritas
Que iban á buscarlo á él.

El dieciseis batallón
Fue su triste paradero,
Que entonces se hallaba á mando,
Del coronel Escudero.

De Orizaba la ciudad,
El día 22 de Mayo,
Fué á la capital mandado
Al Cuartel de la Piedad.

Llegó á la Ciudad de México
¡Amigos que sufrimiento!
Lo visitaba Panchito,
Que marchó en su regimiento.

Llegaron á mis oídos
Todos los sucesos estos......
¡Por una ingrata mujer
Tuvo tantos sufrimientos!

Pedro se llama el amigo
Que compuso este corrido,
¡San Felipe de las maderas!
¡Donde quiera es conocido!

Si quieren saber su nombre,
Juntamente su apellido
Tiene J. K. y H.....
Y del cielo es protejido.

Adiós Juanita querida,
Adiós Luisita y Amada
Adiós mi mamá Dominga
¡Ya te veo muy avanzada!

En fin, yo ya me despido,
Pasando como un ensueño
Ya cantamos el corrido
Del valiente oaxaqueño.

Adiós Luisa, se acabò
La sombra de tu siprés......
¡Esta historia aconteció
En mil novecientos diez!

Imp. de Antonio Vanegas Arroyo, 2a. de Santa Teresa núm. 43. México—1911.

FIG. 9. José Guadalupe Posada (Mexican, 1852–1913). *Corrido of a Brave Oaxacan.* 1911. Relief print on paper, 11 13⁄16 x 15 3⁄4" (30 x 39.9 cm). THE ART INSTITUTE OF CHICAGO. WILLIAM MCCALLIN MCKEE MEMORIAL ENDOWMENT

images with roots in Catholicism) and in particular to ex-voto paintings, which offered up thanks for divine intervention. Often placed in churches and on shrines by worshippers, ex-voto paintings are usually made by untrained artists who find imaginative methods for visually narrating the details of a harrowing ordeal, as well as its miraculous resolution **[FIG. 11]**.

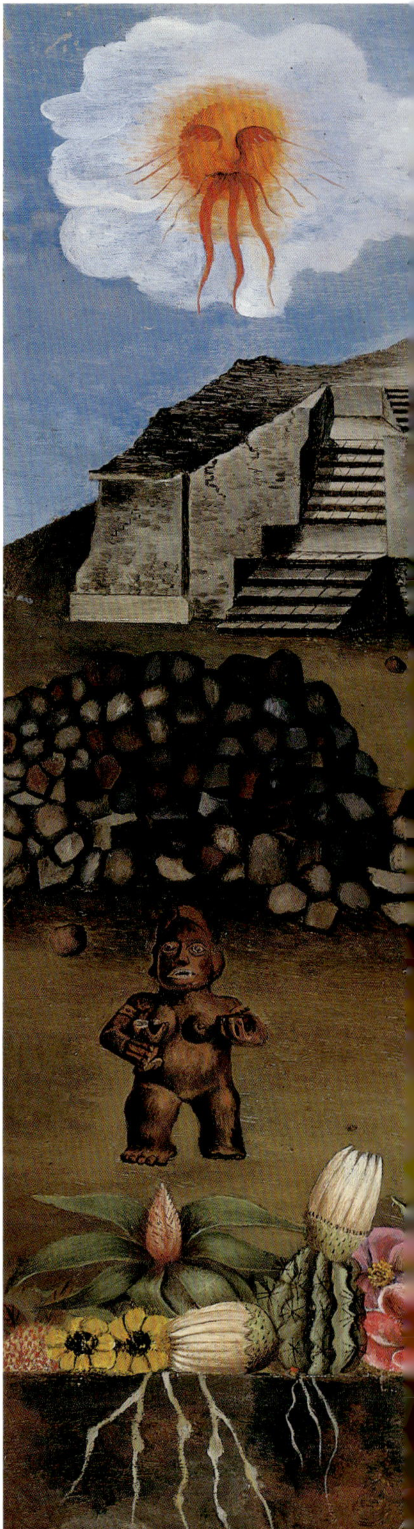

FIG. 10. Frida Kahlo (Mexican, 1907–1954). *Self-Portrait at the Border Line between Mexico and the United States*. 1932. Oil on metal, 12 13⁄16 x 13 13⁄16" (31 x 35 cm). PRIVATE COLLECTION

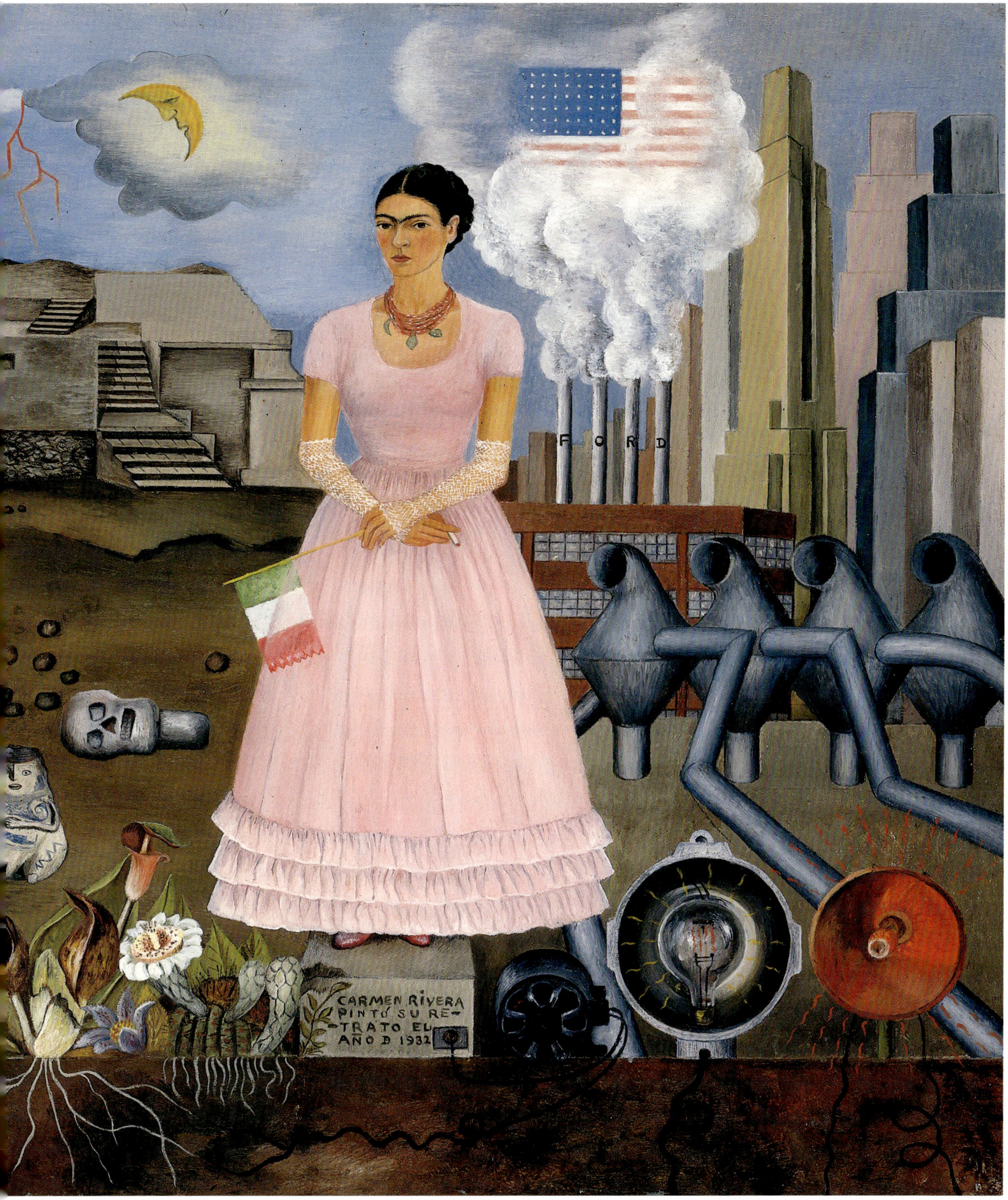
FORD
CARMEN RIVERA
PINTÓ SU RE-
TRATO EL
AÑO D 1932

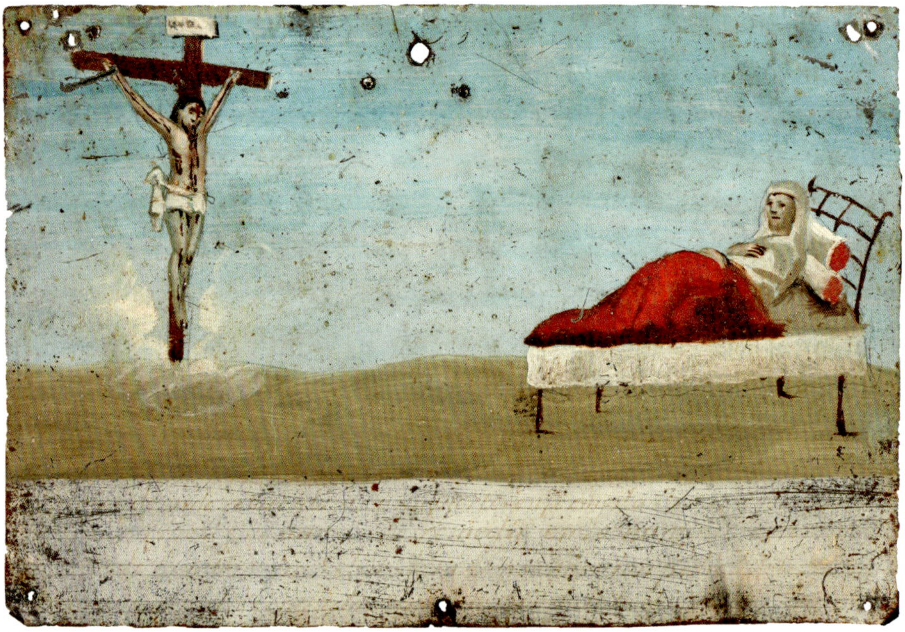

FIG. 11. Artist unknown. Ex-voto. Date unknown. Oil on metal, 7 x 10" (17.8 x 25.4 cm). EL PASO MUSEUM OF ART. GIFT OF NANCY HAMILTON

In both form and function, Kahlo's paintings bring the ex-voto tradition into the realm of modern art. The artist's lack of formal artistic training accounts in part for passages in her paintings that depart from the ideals of illusionism inculcated in art schools. But Kahlo also deliberately cultivated a degree of awkwardness in her paint handling and adopted unorthodox materials as a sign of solidarity with generations of unnamed makers of retablos and ex-voto paintings. The banner-bearing bird in *Frieda and Diego Rivera* **[FIG. 12]**, which disrupts the illusion of the three-dimensional space inhabited by the two figures, for example, harks back to the texts inscribed by the devout on retablos, chronicling the circumstances of a work's making. Kahlo's paintings on metal, such as *Henry Ford Hospital* **[FIG. 13]**, are a nod to ex-voto painters, who often favored a hard, metallic surface. Even the nondescript setting of *Self-Portrait with Cropped Hair*, a no-man's-land composed only of a stark horizon line dividing brown ground from mottled sky, is reminiscent of ex-voto scenes in which figures and objects take precedence over realistic descriptions of place.

FIG. 12. Frida Kahlo (Mexican, 1907–1954). *Frieda and Diego Rivera*. 1931. Oil on canvas, 39 ⅜ x 31" (100 x 78.7 cm). SAN FRANCISCO MUSEUM OF MODERN ART. ALBERT M. BENDER COLLECTION, GIFT OF ALBERT M. BENDER

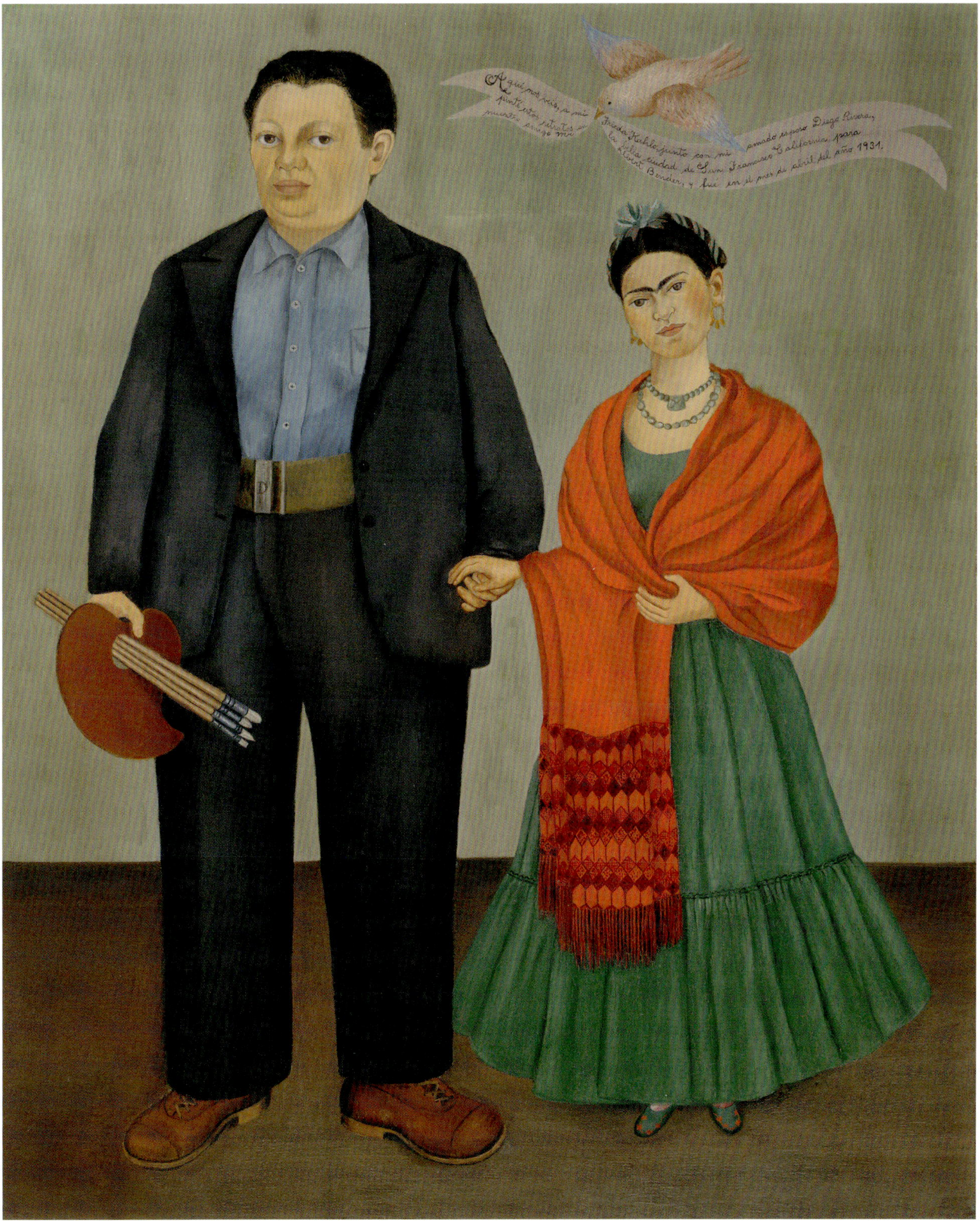
Aquí nos veis, a mí Frieda Kahlo, junto con mi amado esposo Diego Rivera,
pinté estos retratos en la bella ciudad de San Francisco California para
nuestro amigo Mr. Albert Bender, y fué en el mes de abril del año 1931.

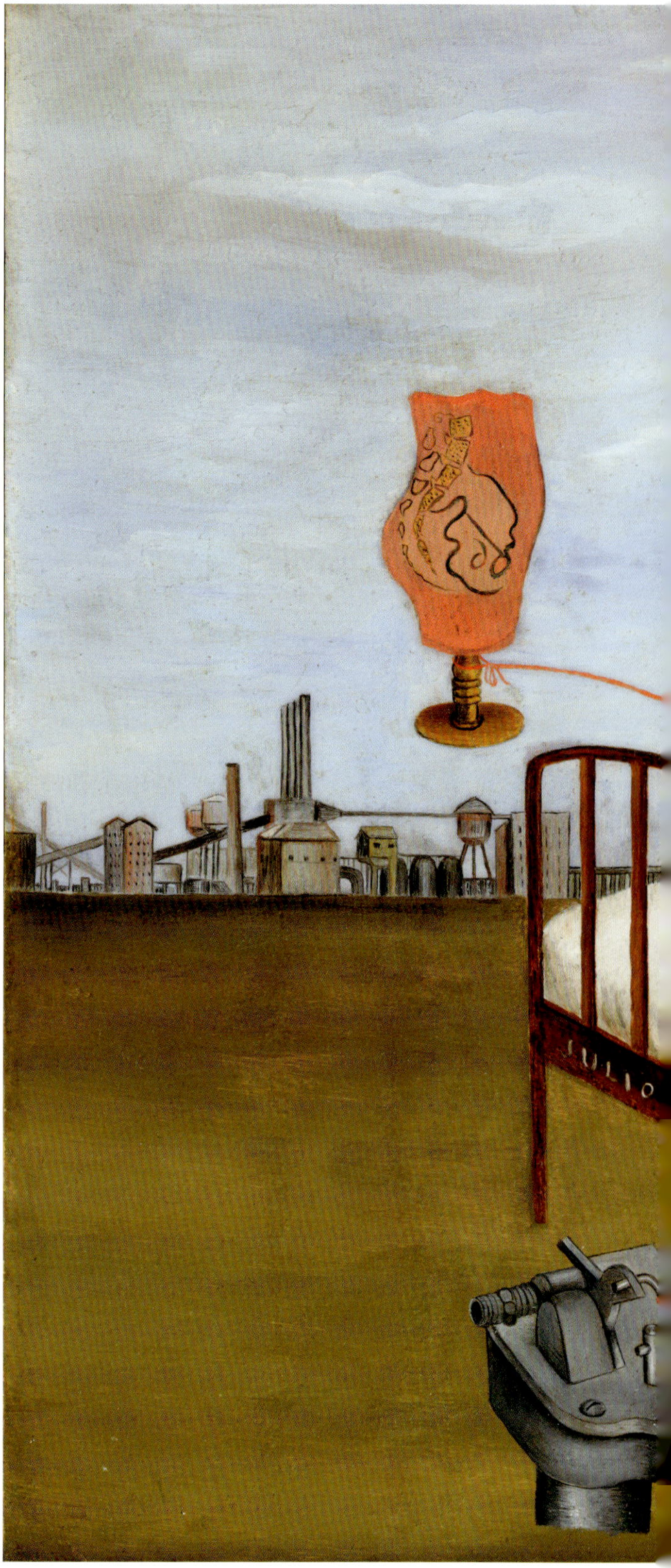

FIG. 13. Frida Kahlo (Mexican, 1907–1954). *Henry Ford Hospital.* 1932. Oil on metal, 11$\frac{13}{16}$ x 15" (30 x 38 cm). MUSEO DOLORES OLMEDO, MEXICO CITY

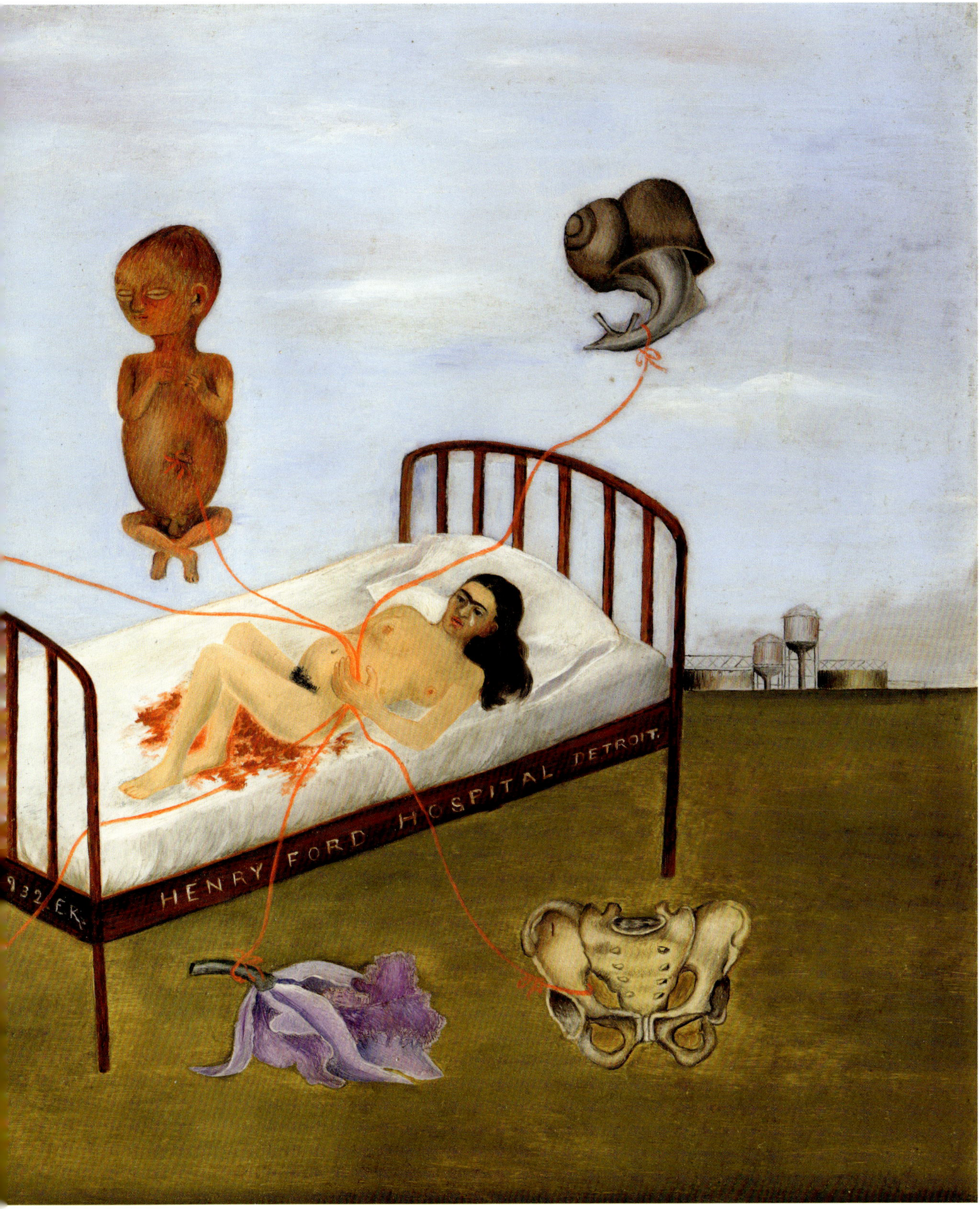

HENRY FORD HOSPITAL DETROIT.
932. F.K.

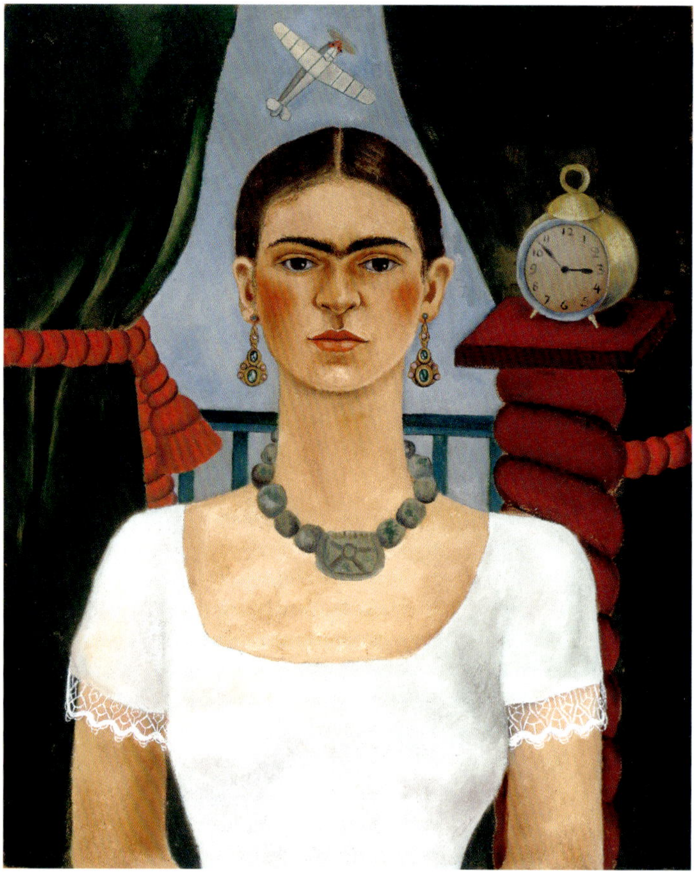

FIG. 14. Frida Kahlo. *Self-Portrait (Time Flies)*. 1929. Oil on Masonite, 30 ½ x 24" (77.5 x 61 cm). PRIVATE COLLECTION

Beyond her painting techniques and materials, Kahlo's own body and its ornamentation were central to her exploration of *mexicanidad*. In her self-portraits Kahlo oscillates between presenting herself in European or U.S. fashions and styling herself as an artifact of Mexican history.[5] The fusion of cultural referents in *Self-Portrait (Time Flies)* **[FIG. 14]**—white peasant blouse, gold colonial-era earrings, Mayan jade necklace—attests to her omnivorous appetite for appropriation and play.[6] But by the late 1930s Kahlo had begun to home in on a favorite Mexican type: the Tehuana, a woman from the isthmus of Tehuantepec, in southern Mexico, the heartland of the ancient Zapotec empire. The Tehuana costume, consisting of a boxy blouse and flowing skirt, at times embellished with designs in embroidery and ribbon, stood in deliberate contrast, for Kahlo, to Western feminine fashions, such as the elaborate Victorian blouse in *The Two Fridas* **[FIG. 15]**.

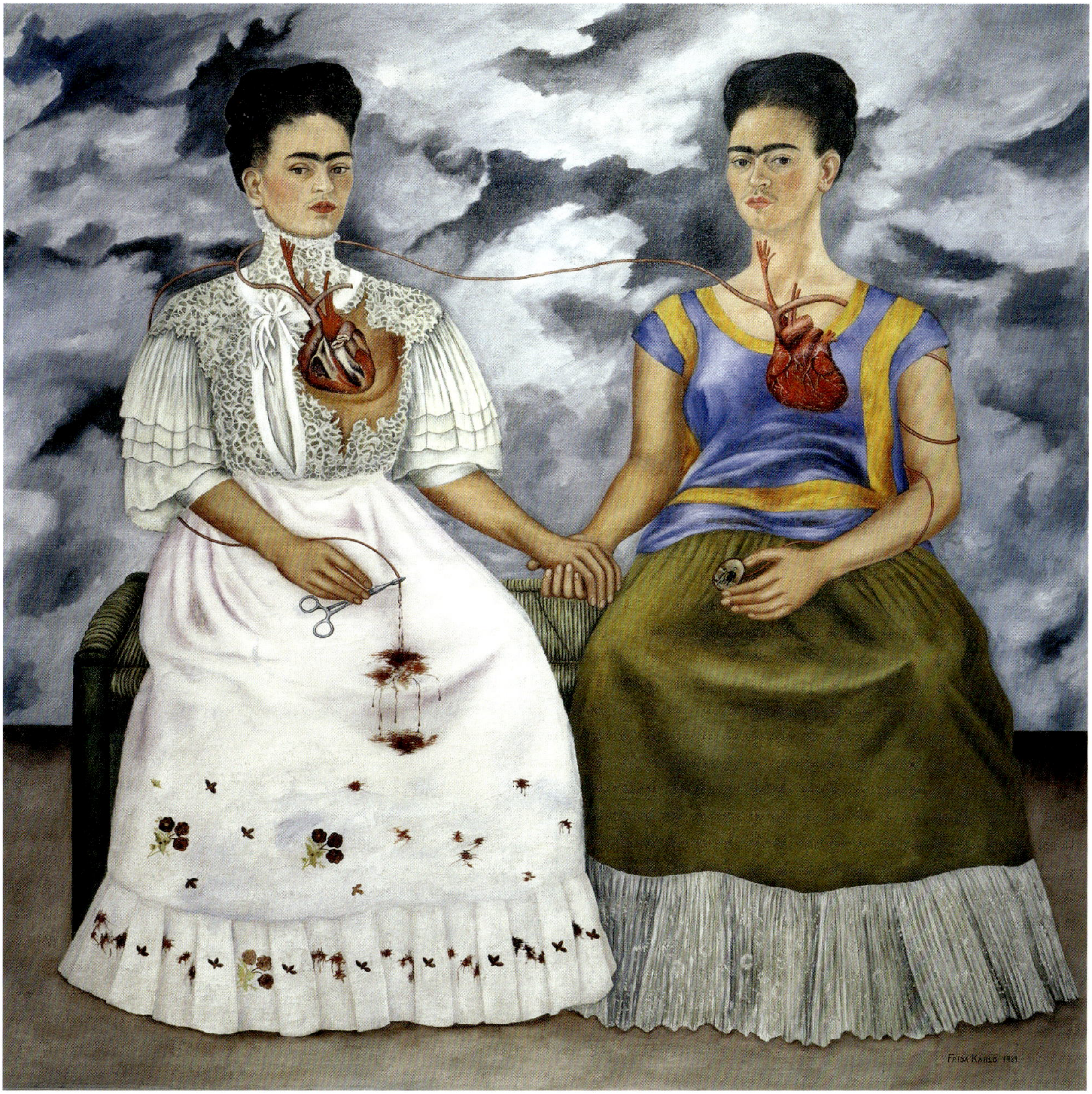

FIG. 15. Frida Kahlo (Mexican, 1907–1954). *The Two Fridas*. 1939. Oil on canvas, 68 5⁄16 x 68 1⁄8" (173.5 x 173 cm). MUSEO DE ARTE MODERNO, MEXICO CITY

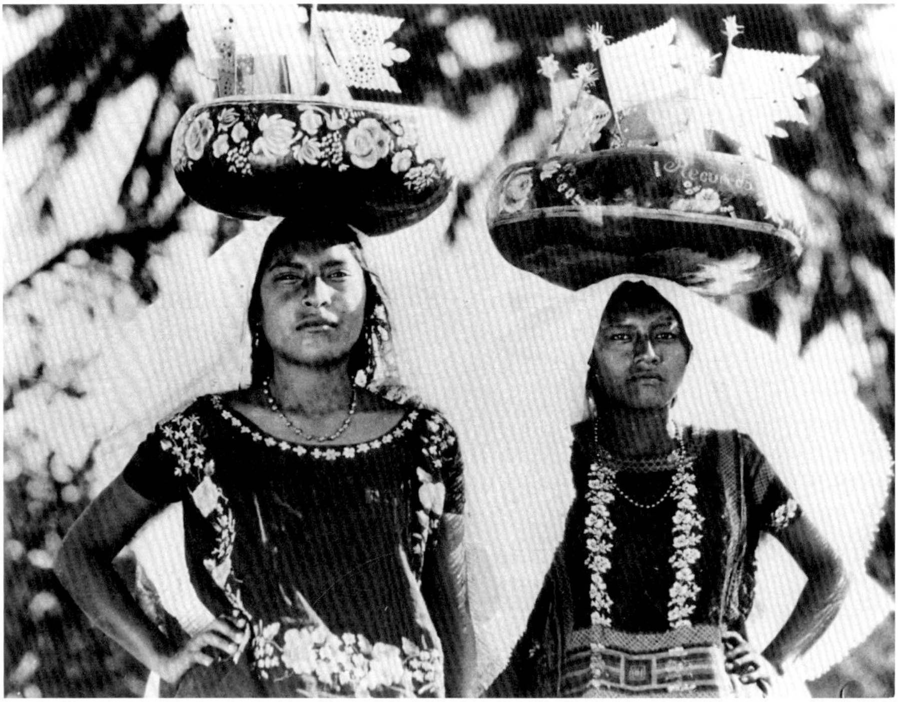

FIG. 16. Sergei Eisenstein (Russian, 1898–1948). *¡Que Viva Mexico!* 1930–32. 35mm film (black and white, silent), unedited footage. THE MUSEUM OF MODERN ART, NEW YORK. GIFT OF UPTON SINCLAIR

The women of Tehuantepec were famous for the economic and political power they wielded in their matriarchal society. After the revolution, the Tehuana became a symbol of self-sufficiency, resistance to the pressures of colonialism and assimilation, and, for artists such as Kahlo, female autonomy.[7] Kahlo was not alone in training her eye on the Tehuana. This regional identity, for leftist artists in particular, seemed to stand as evidence of Mexico's capacity for developing and maintaining social structures distinct from the hierarchical and exploitative systems born of colonialist expansion and capitalist drive. Rivera made these women an essential theme in his SEP murals, and the Soviet filmmaker Sergei Eisenstein came away from the region, after traveling there in 1930, with reels of footage for his landmark unfinished film *¡Que viva Mexico!* (1930–32; **FIG. 16**). In a move that most closely approximated Kahlo's adoption of the indigenous identity, the Italian-born photographer Tina Modotti pictured herself in Tehuana garb while on a trip to photograph the women of Tehuantepec [**FIG. 17**].

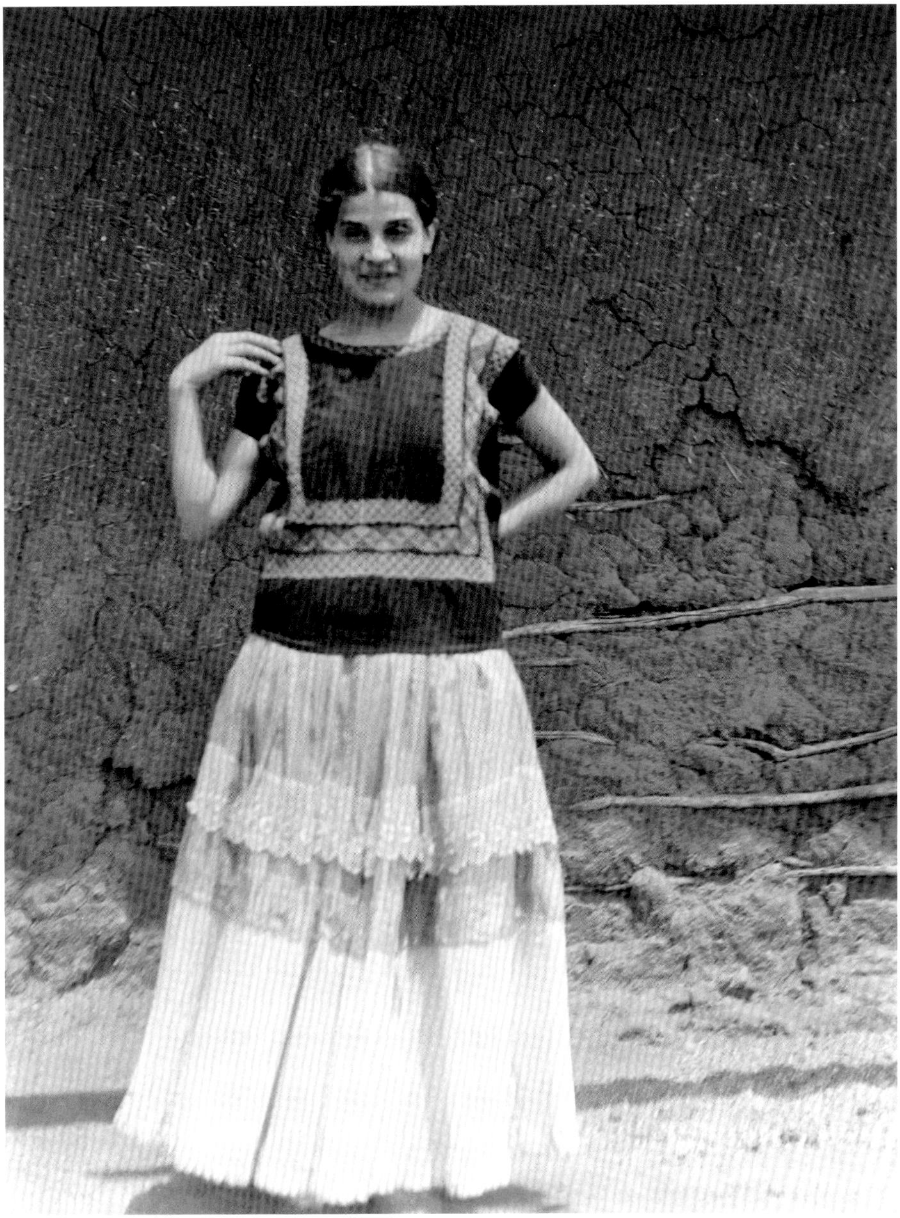

FIG. 17. Tina Modotti (Italian, 1896–1942). *Untitled ("Costume from Tehuantepec")*. n.d. Gelatin silver print, 3 ½ x 2 ½" (8.9 x 6.4 cm). SAN FRANCISCO MUSEUM OF MODERN ART. PURCHASE THROUGH A GIFT OF THE ART SUPPORTING FOUNDATION, JOHN "LAUNNY" STEFFENS, SANDRA LLOYD, SHAWN AND BROOK BYERS, MR. AND MRS. GEORGE F. JEWETT, JR., AND ANONYMOUS DONORS

In light of Kahlo's intense exploration of *mexicanidad* in the 1920s and '30s, the lack of explicit references to her home country in *Self-Portrait with Cropped Hair* appears particularly radical. Only the keenest of inspections reveals signs of her recent Mexicanist pursuits: the song inscribed at the top of the work hints at the time and place in which the painting was made; the ends of the artist's long braids make an unobtrusive appearance (one has fallen on the floor near her chair, the other lies limp across her knee); and some scholars have seen signs of Kahlo's interest in Mexican folk art in the bright-yellow wicker chair she sits upon **[FIG. 18]**.[8] Yet the lexicon of signs Kahlo carefully crafted in the first decade of her career to signal devotion to her home country—references to pre-Columbian culture and Mexico's natural landscape, the use of regional costumes—are most conspicuous for their absence.

The identity switch proposed in the painting took aim squarely at Rivera, an artist inseparable from the high *mexicanista* fervor of the 1920s and early '30s. The work describes an act of revenge: Kahlo has rid herself of the Mexicanist stylings she had adopted, with Rivera's strong approval, over the course of the late 1920s and early 1930s and instead affects a male presentation so stereotypical and general as to defy association with a particular time or place. Kahlo accuses Rivera of superficiality, implying with the song lyrics that his love for her failed to extend beyond the nativist Mexican features she carefully cultivated in her appearance and artwork, characteristics that accorded with his own artistic ideology. In suddenly erasing the outward signs of her Mexicanness in *Self-Portrait with Cropped Hair*, Kahlo seems to issue a withering critique of her romantic partner and at the same time acknowledge such signs as symbols to be taken up or dismissed at will—socially conditioned signifiers rather than endemic traits.

The new identity Kahlo adopts in *Self-Portrait with Cropped Hair* is as important as the one she gives up. Given the bulky proportions of the suit in the painting, scholars have often assumed that it is Rivera's, in which case her donning of it might be read as an attempt to close a physical and emotional distance between her and her partner.[9] In fact, Kahlo had previously used clothing to flout conventional gender roles and power relations. As a teenager she shocked her conservative family members by dressing in a man's three-piece suit for family photographs **[FIG. 19]**. She was notorious for smoking, drinking heavily,

OPPOSITE: FIG. 18. Frida Kahlo (Mexican, 1907–1954). *Self-Portrait with Cropped Hair* (detail). 1940

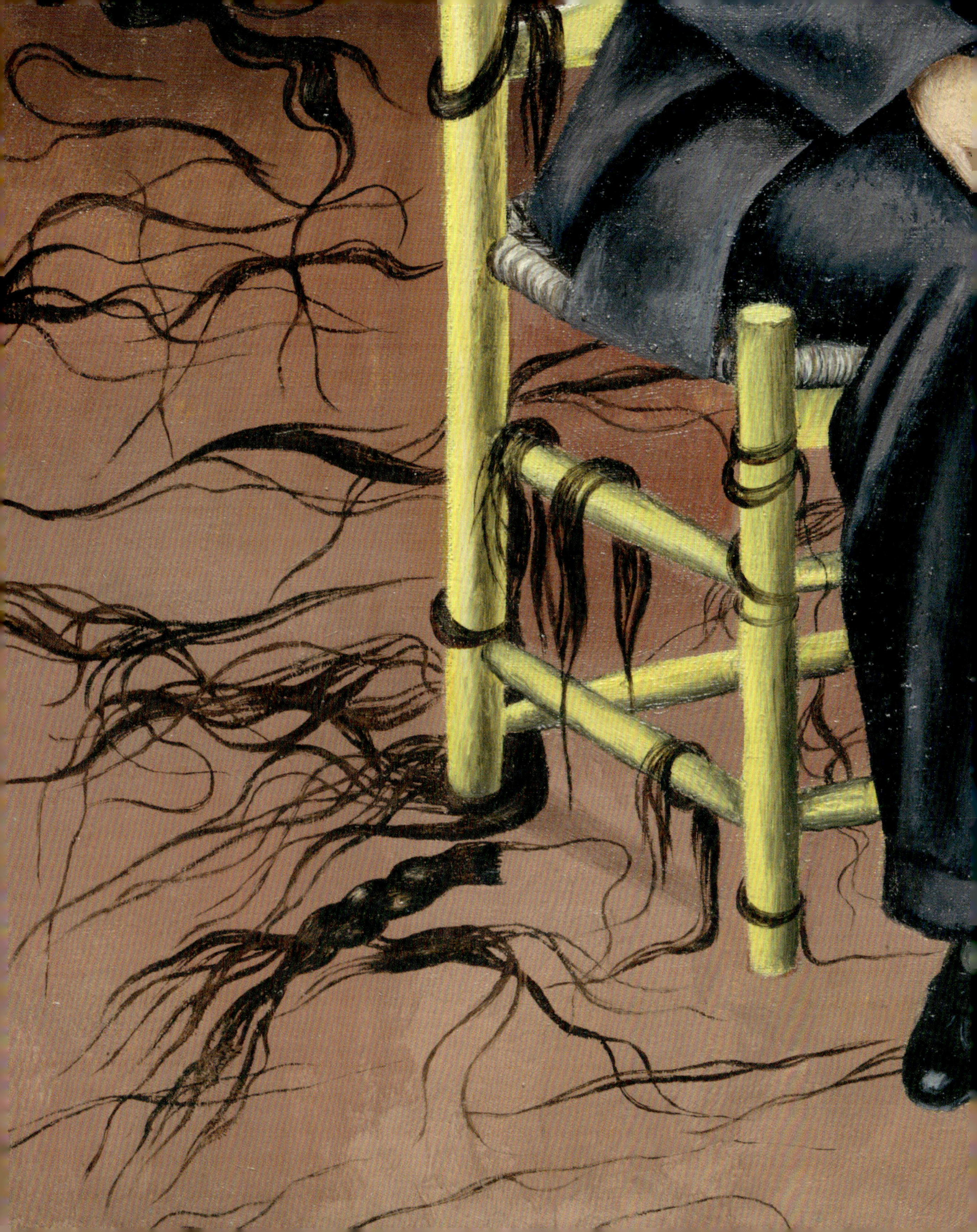

FIG. 19. Family portrait, with Kahlo at left, by Guillermo Kahlo, 1926.
VICENTE WOLF COLLECTION

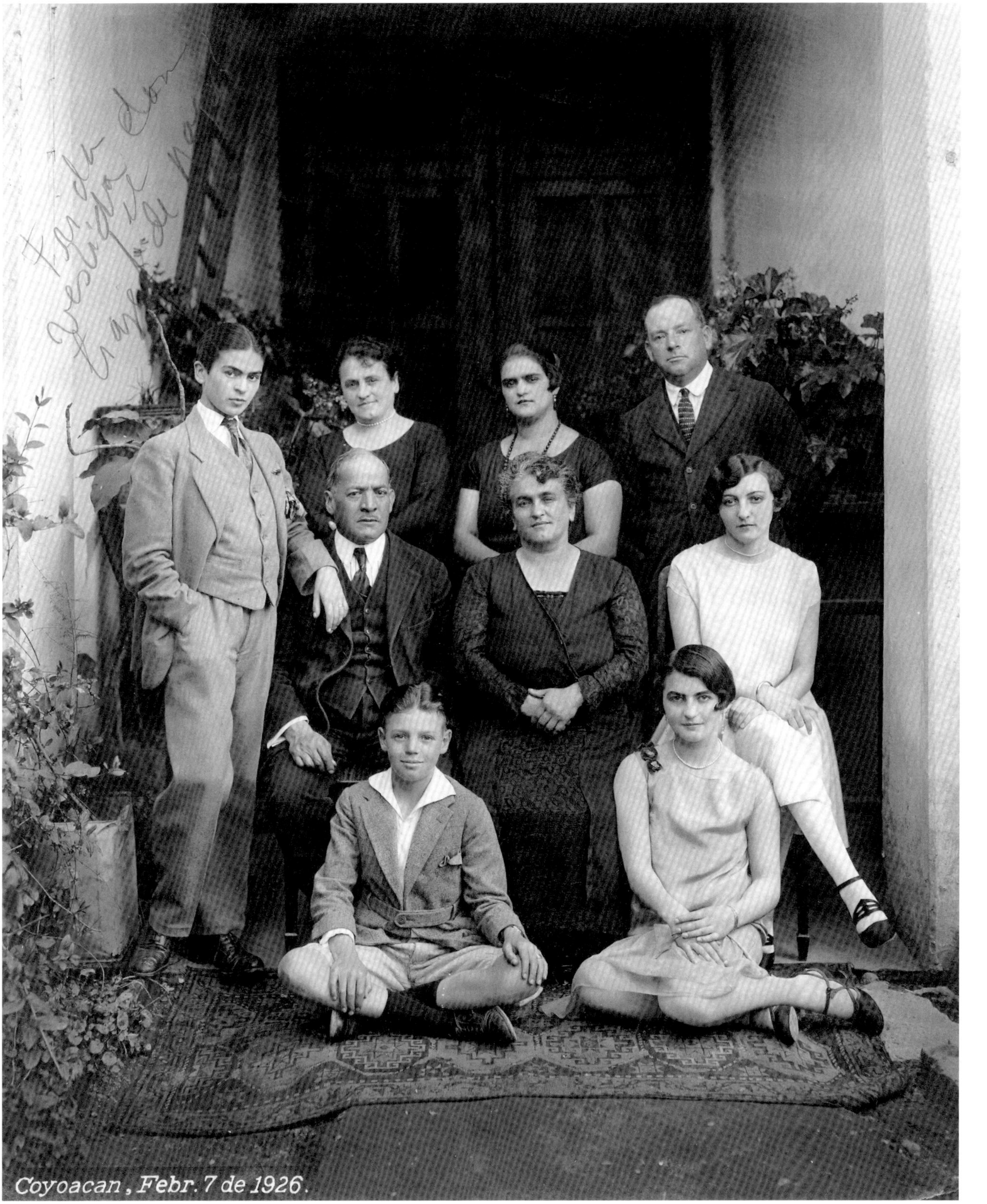
Coyoacan, Febr. 7 de 1926.

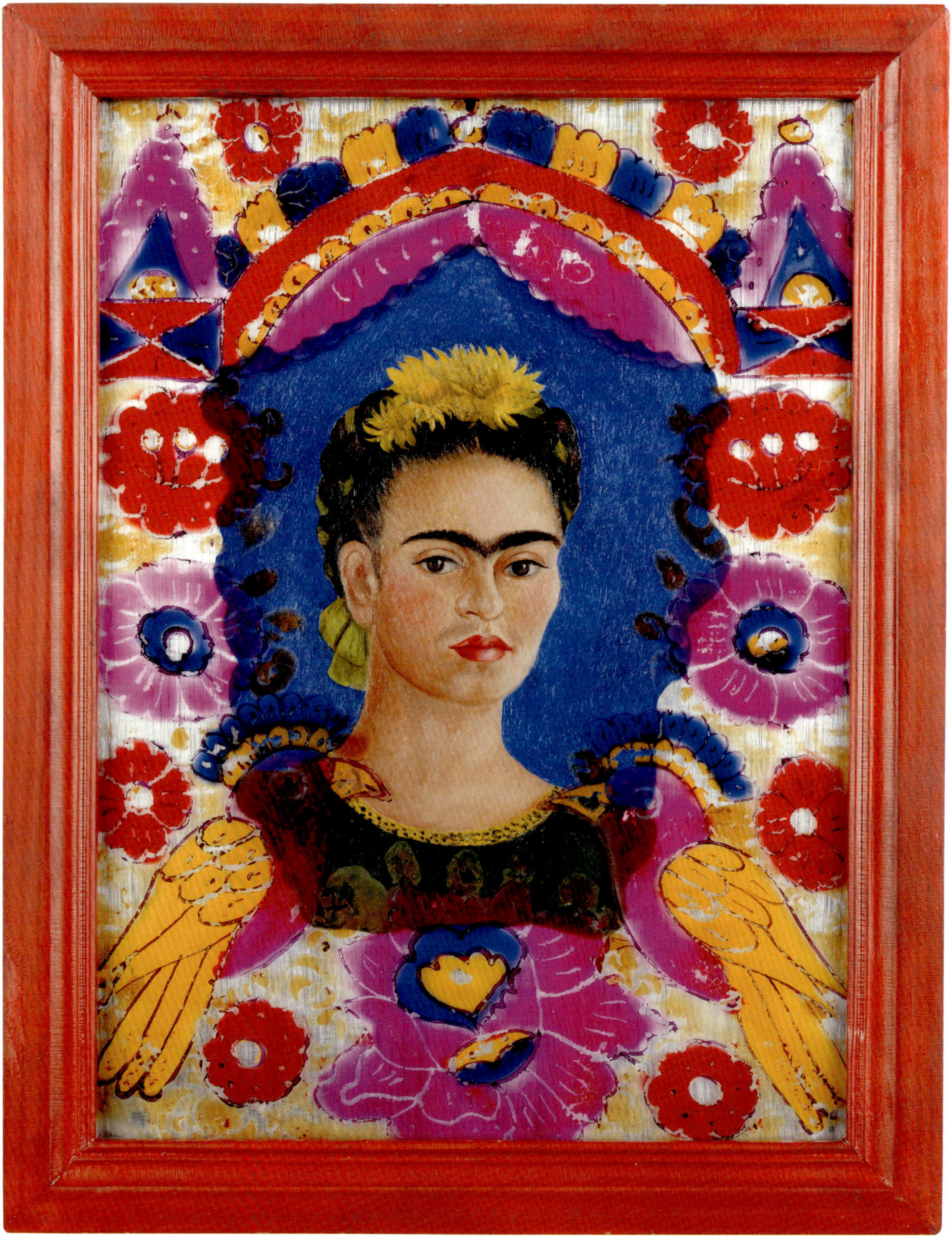

cursing enthusiastically in multiple languages, and pursuing romantic relationships with both men and women—all behaviors that defied contemporary standards of ladylike comportment. She was also acutely aware of the difficulties women artists faced in pursuing a professional career: as the wife of a globetrotting celebrity painter, Kahlo was often described in the press as Rivera's exotic, diminutive sidekick, a Sunday painter with few professional claims of her own. He, by contrast, was celebrated for his virility and outsized ambition. Rather than simply a sign of longing for Rivera, Kahlo's decision to dress as a man indicated her own growing ambition and an increasing desire to inhabit an art world dominated by men. Unlike the ex-voto, which credits a supernatural power with the solving of a problem, *Self-Portrait with Cropped Hair* positions Kahlo as the agent of her own healing and growth, through a radical reinvention of self.

Indeed, in the late 1930s, just before her divorce from Rivera, Kahlo's work had begun to draw attention in the United States and Europe. She traveled to New York for an exhibition at Julien Levy Gallery in November 1938, at which almost half of the paintings sold and whose opening was attended by such luminaries as Isamu Noguchi and Georgia O'Keeffe.[10] The following spring she was the star of an exhibition at Galerie Renou & Colle, in Paris. Her work caught the eye of new patrons, including A. Conger Goodyear, a founder of The Museum of Modern Art; the actor and art collector Edward G. Robinson; and the writer and future politician Clare Boothe Luce.[11] In Paris, Kahlo mixed with artists such as Wassily Kandinsky, Pablo Picasso, and Marcel Duchamp, and the Louvre acquired one of her self-portraits **[FIG. 20]**.

These successes coincided with Kahlo's entrée into international Surrealism. Her association with the movement was solidified when André Breton, its self-appointed leader, became infatuated with her during a trip to Mexico in 1938. Breton had traveled there with the support of the French ministry of foreign affairs to give a series of lectures; beyond this professional obligation, he was looking forward to meeting Rivera, whose work he already knew, and Leon Trotsky, the Russian revolutionary who had been living in exile in Mexico since 1936 **[FIG. 21]**. Breton was also eager to explore a country whose history and culture had captured his imagination as a child. As an adult, he felt that Mexico offered an alternative to Europe's stultifying cultural limitations.

FIG. 20. Frida Kahlo (Mexican, 1907–1954). *The Frame*. 1938. Oil on metal and glass, 11 ¼ x 8 3⁄16" (28.5 x 20.7 cm). MUSÉE NATIONAL D'ART MODERNE, CENTRE POMPIDOU, PARIS

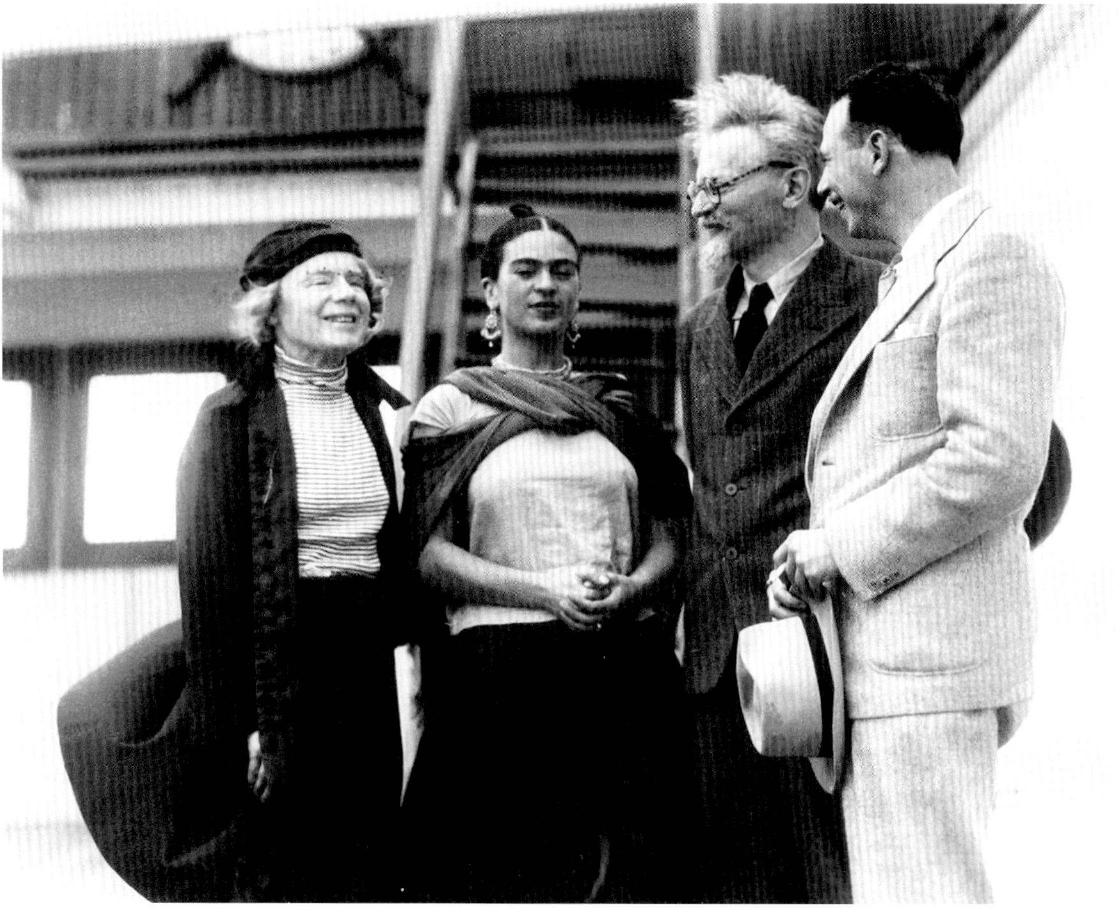

FIG. 21. Kahlo, with the pro-union activist Max Shachtman (at far right), greets Leon Trotsky and his wife Natalia Sedova on their arrival in Mexico, January 9, 1937

With the publication of the first Surrealist manifesto, in 1924, Breton called for war on a Western tradition that he denounced as corrupt, crippled by its unwavering faith in rational thinking, and utterly lacking in imagination. Surrealism would provide a path forward, a new way of thinking that would break free of tired post-Enlightenment values by tapping into the unconscious mind. In a fluctuating group of writers and artists linked by their interest in the movement's central tenets rather than by a particular style or approach to art making, the Surrealists created works that embraced the marvelous and the irrational in pursuit of new psychological insights. Many in the group, including Breton, championed cultures untouched by European thinking as models of authenticity. The Surrealists maintained the belief that the indigenous cultures of Oceania, Africa, and the Americas accepted irrationality, mystery, and the darker side of the human psyche more readily than so-called civilized societies, thus allowing them a more genuine and holistic connection to the unconscious. Freighted with preconceived notions of what Mexico—home to numerous pre-Columbian empires—would be, Breton unsurprisingly and gleefully declared the country to be the "surrealist place par excellence" after spending only a short time there. "At no time until the present," he wrote of his trip in the Surrealist journal *Minotaure* in 1939, "has the splendor of reality surpassed the promise of dreams."[12]

Breton promoted Kahlo's paintings as quintessential manifestations of Mexico's supposedly innate surrealism. In an essay written for the Julien Levy exhibition, he claimed that her work was "pure surreality"—despite "[having] been conceived without any prior knowledge whatsoever of the ideas motivating the activities of my friends and myself."[13] *Portrait of Luther Burbank* **[FIG. 22]**, for example, contemplates the limitations of human existence with a subject

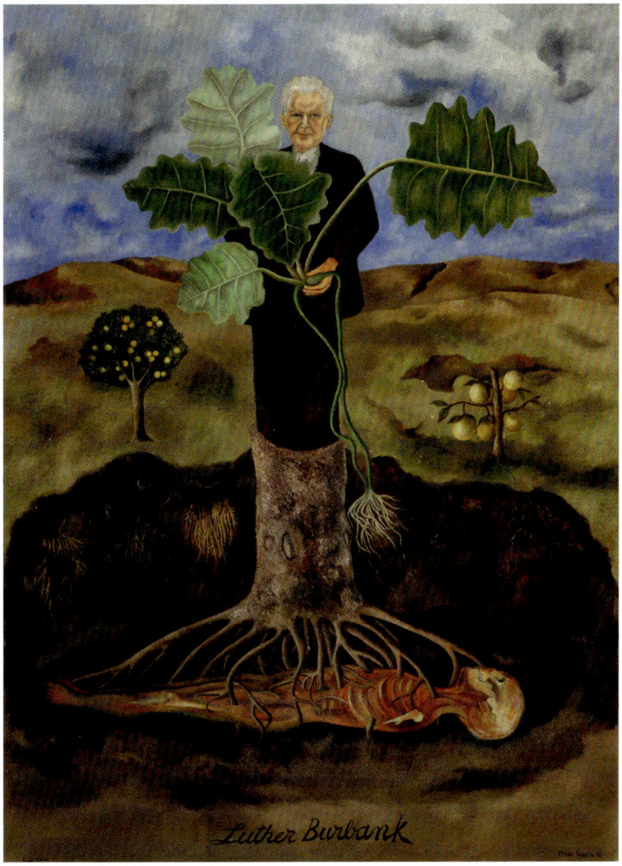

FIG. 22. Frida Kahlo (Mexican, 1907–1954). *Portrait of Luther Burbank*. 1931. Oil on Masonite, 34 ¼ x 24 7⁄16" (87 x 62 cm). MUSEO DOLORES OLMEDO, MEXICO CITY

that mysteriously transmutates between human and vegetal forms. In *The Four Inhabitants of Mexico City* **[FIG. 23]**, Mexico's pre-Columbian past coexists with folk customs of the present. In *What the Water Gave Me* **[FIG. 24]**, the magical and the literal intermingle in space and time.

Breton helped establish the terms by which international viewers understood Kahlo's work and the context in which it was made, suggesting that her art, her persona, and Mexico's long history converged to affirm the transnational and transhistorical validity of Surrealism. Breton's proclamation that Kahlo herself was "like a fairy-tale princess, with magic spells at her finger-tips . . . an apparition in the flash of light of the *quetzal* bird which scatters opals among the rocks as it flies away" no doubt had an impact—on Levy, for example, who described her as a "mythical creature, not of this world."[14] The reviews of the New York show reiterated this fascination with Kahlo's exoticism and insisted on her naivete and untainting by European artistic training. Her works "had the daintiness of miniatures," wrote a critic in *Time*, with "the vivid reds and yellows of Mexican tradition and the playfully bloody fancy of an unsentimental child."[15] In *Vogue*, Kahlo's friend Bertram D. Wolfe described her paintings as "a sort of 'naïve' Surrealism, which she invented for herself"; her works, further, were not

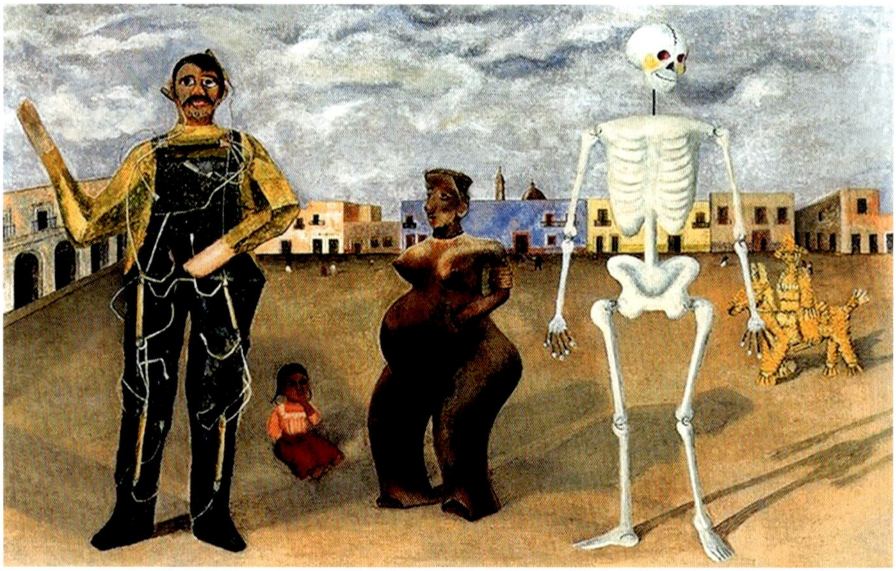

FIG. 23. Frida Kahlo (Mexican, 1907–1954). *The Four Inhabitants of Mexico City*. 1937. Oil on metal, 12 ¾ x 18 ¾" (32.4 x 47.6 cm). PRIVATE COLLECTION

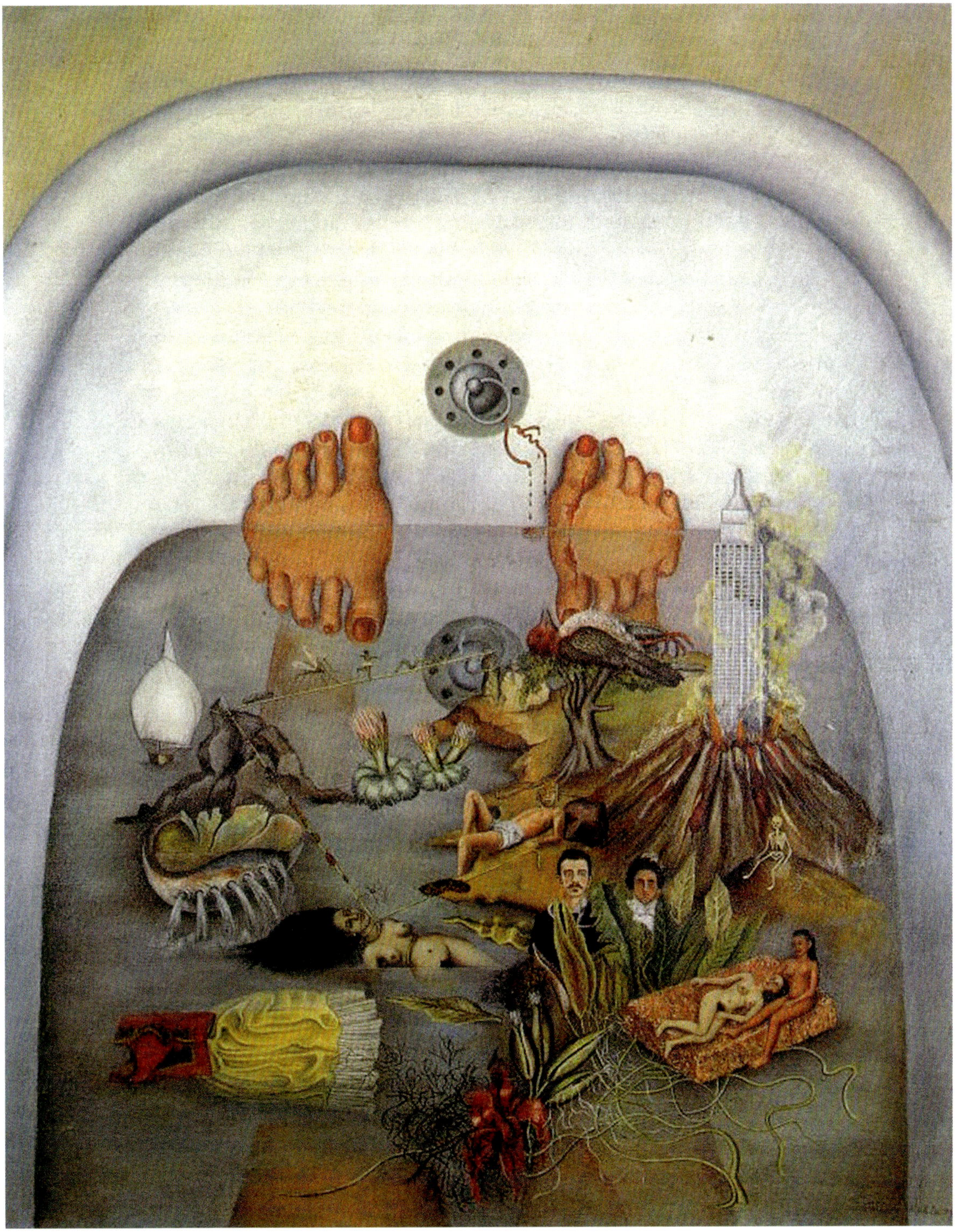

FIG. 24. Frida Kahlo (Mexican, 1907–1954). *What the Water Gave Me*. 1938. Oil on canvas, 34 ⅝ x 27 $^{3}/_{16}$" (88 x 69 cm). DANIEL FILIPACCHI COLLECTION, PARIS

weighed down by the "Freudian symbols and philosophy that obsess the official Surrealist painters."[16] Breton continued to blur the distinctions between Kahlo, her paintings, and Mexico, all the while maintaining that her work was distinct from that of his European colleagues. Without her consent, he added examples of Mexican folk art and photographs by Manuel Álvarez Bravo to her exhibition at Galerie Renou & Colle **[FIG. 25]**. This sort of curatorial decision, which undermines the artist's creative agency and the public's perception of it, posited Kahlo as an artist passively shaped by her surroundings rather than by her own will and intellectual curiosity.

Kahlo's pushed back against Breton's overdetermined view of her in ways both overt and subtle. In the press release for the Levy show, she adopted a tone of mock deference, quipping, "I never knew I was a Surrealist until André Breton came to Mexico and told me I was one," and hinted that she preferred to keep the possibilities for self-definition open: "I myself still don't know what I am."[17] In later years, Kahlo acknowledged the common ground her work shared with the artists who willingly wore the Surrealist mantle, while also demanding

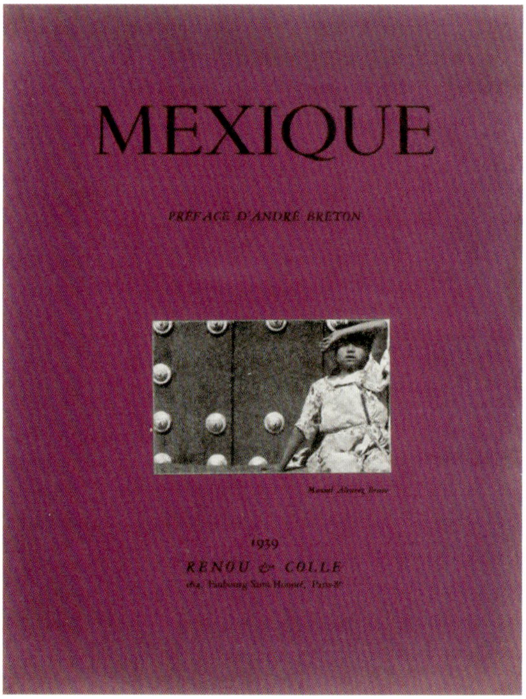

FIG. 25. Cover of the exhibition catalogue for *Mexique* (1939), at Galerie Renou & Colle, Paris. ASSOCIATION ATELIER ANDRÉ BRETON

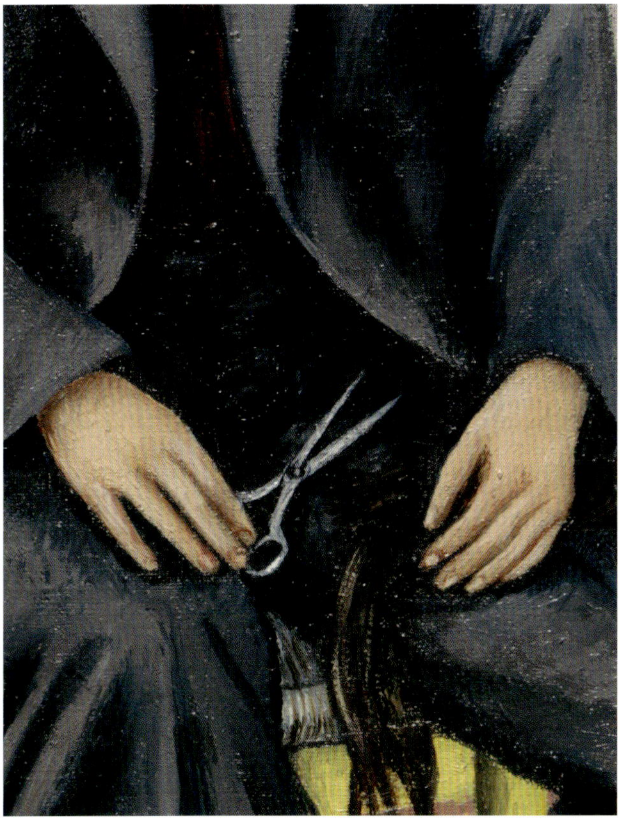

FIG. 26. Frida Kahlo (Mexican, 1907–1954). *Self-Portrait with Cropped Hair* (detail). 1940

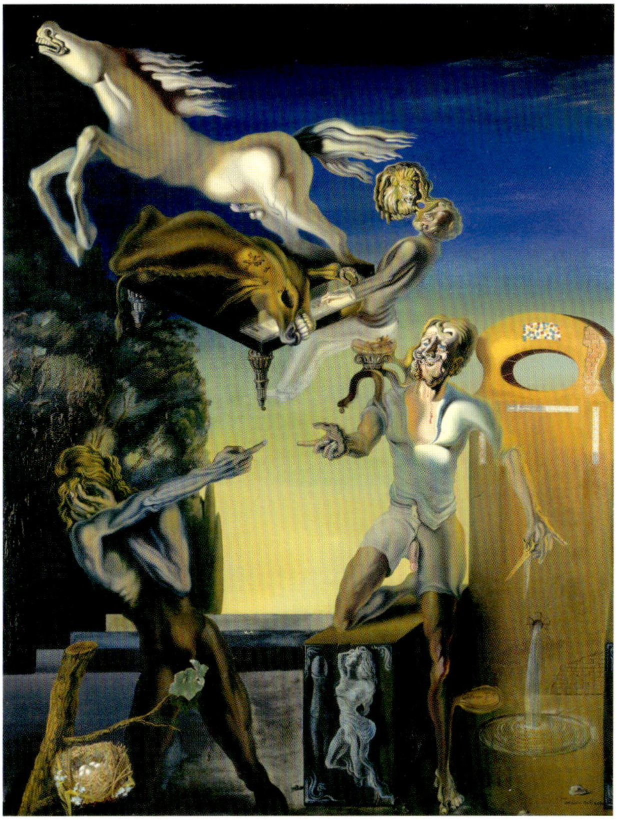

FIG. 27. Salvador Dalí (Spanish, 1904–1989). *Guillaume Tell*. 1930. Oil and collage on canvas, 44 ½ x 34 ¼" (113 x 87 cm). CENTRE POMPIDOU, PARIS. PURCHASED WITH THE HELP OF FONDS DU PATRIMOINE

recognition of her creative self-determination. "I adore surprise and the unexpected," she explained, "and it is doubtless true that in many ways my painting is related to that of the Surrealists. But I never had the intention of creating a work that could be considered to fit in that classification."[18]

Self-Portrait with Cropped Hair, in making clear Kahlo's understanding of Surrealist symbolism, contains a rebuke of the movement's tendency to treat her as childlike and exotic. The careful position of the scissors in front of Kahlo's genitalia is among the most direct representations of castration anxiety in twentieth-century painting **[FIG. 26]**. According to Sigmund Freud, whose writings were central to Surrealist thinking, the primal fear of such damage could lead to intense emotional instability and feelings of powerlessness. Through the work of artists such as Salvador Dalí **[FIG. 27]**, castration anxiety became a favorite among the Surrealists' collection of psychoanalytic themes. The unnerving hair that seems to move independently about Kahlo's painting is another

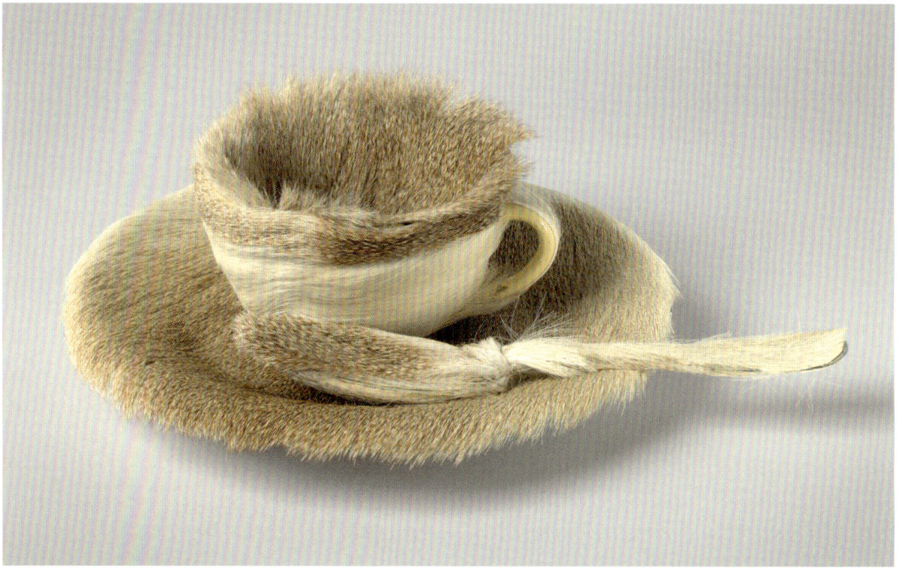

FIG. 28. Meret Oppenehim Oppenheim (Swiss, 1913–1985). *Object* (*Le Déjeuner en fourrure*). 1936. Fur-covered cup, saucer, and spoon, cup: 4 ⅜" (10.9 cm) diam.; saucer 9 ⅜" (23.7 cm) diam.; spoon 8" (20.2 cm) long, overall height 2 ⅞" (7.3 cm) high. THE MUSEUM OF MODERN ART, NEW YORK. PURCHASE

Surrealist trope. A charged, often fetishized anatomical feature, hair is capable of simultaneously attracting and repelling, of inciting both desire and disgust, as Meret Oppenheim so thoroughly demonstrated in *Object* (1936; **FIG. 28**).

Although women had occupied Surrealist circles from the start—and the group as a whole decried the narrow bourgeois ideal of the woman as obedient wife and devoted mother—the movement's most vocal proponents, especially Breton, found it difficult to digest the idea of female artists as independent creative and intellectual forces or complex beings.[19] He made this limited understanding of female subjectivity clear in his comments on Kahlo's work. "I would like to add now that there is no art more exclusively feminine," Breton said of her work, "in the sense that, in order to be as seductive as possible, it is only too willing to play alternately at being absolutely pure and absolutely pernicious."[20] In the writings and artworks of male Surrealists, women appear in a limited number of opposing guises: the mischievous *femme-infant*, the ethereal muse, the sensuous seductress, the captivating femme fatale. These categories of female existence were defined only in terms of their relationship to dominant male subjects and the ways in which they either enhanced or threatened that subject's ego.

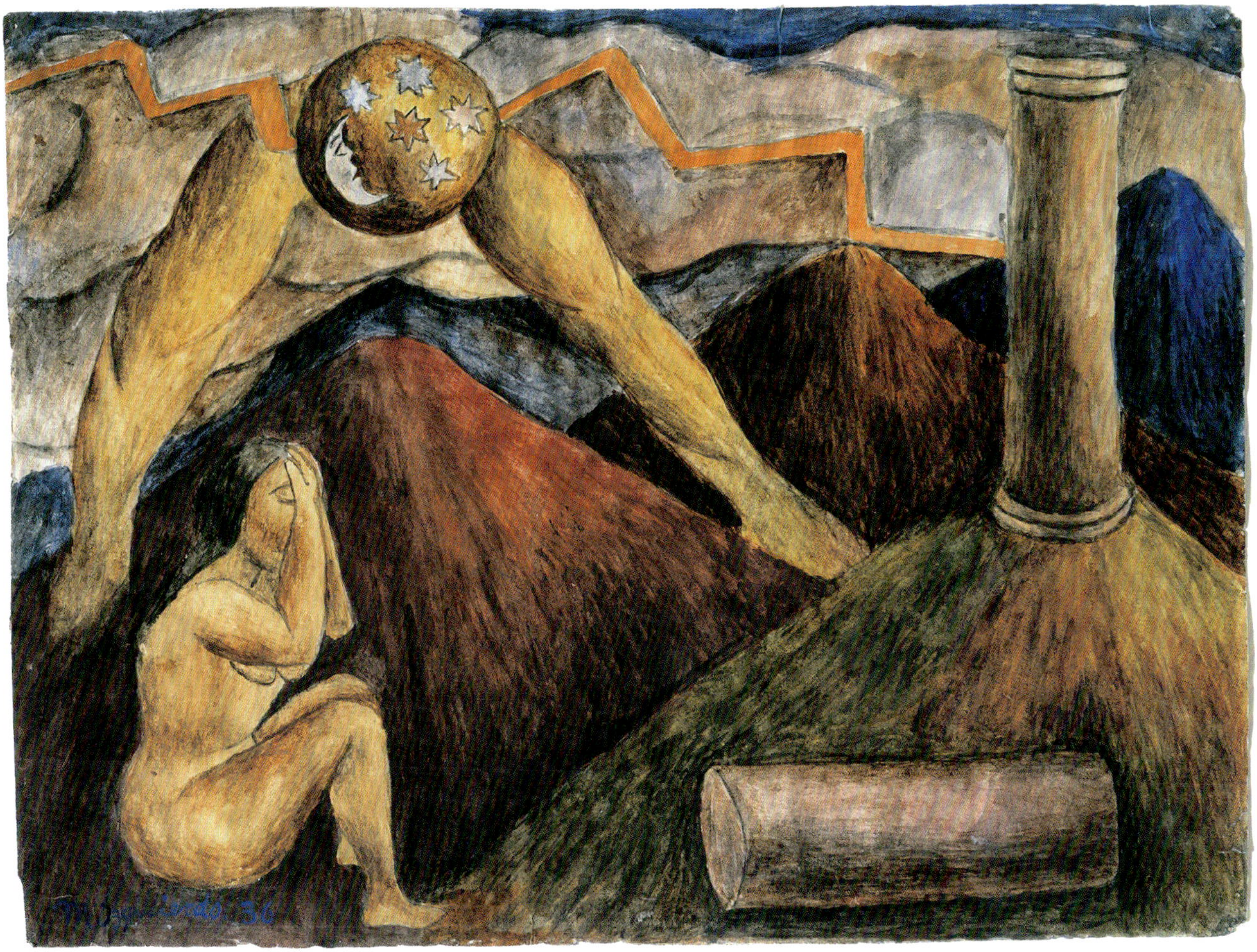

FIG. 29. María Izquierdo. *Allegory of Work*. 1936. Watercolor and tempera on paper, 8 ¼ x 10¹³⁄₁₆" (21 x 27.5 cm). COLLECIÓN ANDRÉS BLAISTEN, MEXICO

Kahlo was not the only female artist in the male-centric world of international Surrealism, and Mexico in the first half of the twentieth century was a locus of women working in a Surrealist vein. These included María Izquierdo, who began painting nudes in fantastic landscapes **[FIG. 29]** in the 1930s and whose works were among the "discoveries" of the French writer Antonin Artaud, who promoted them in Paris after meeting her in Mexico in 1936. The Spanish-born painter Remedios Varo immigrated to Mexico during World War II and began painting dreamlike scenes inspired by alchemy and the occult that were

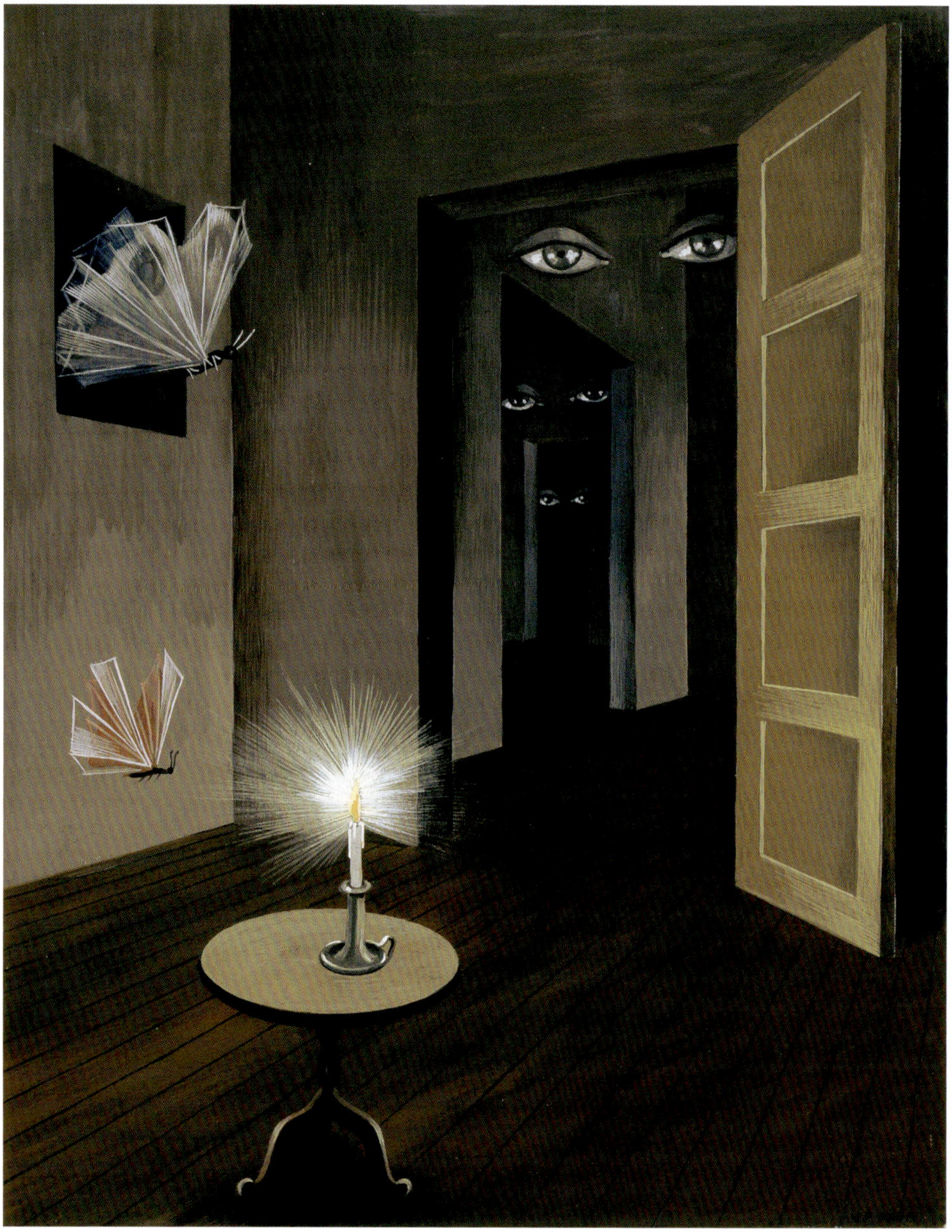

FIG. 30. Remedios Varo (Spanish, 1908–1963). *Insomnia I* (*Insomnio I*). 1947. Gouache on paper, 11 1⁄16 x 8 5⁄8" (28 x 22 cm). THE VERA AND ARTURO SCHWARZ COLLECTION OF DADA AND SURREALIST ART IN THE ISRAEL MUSEUM, JERUSALEM

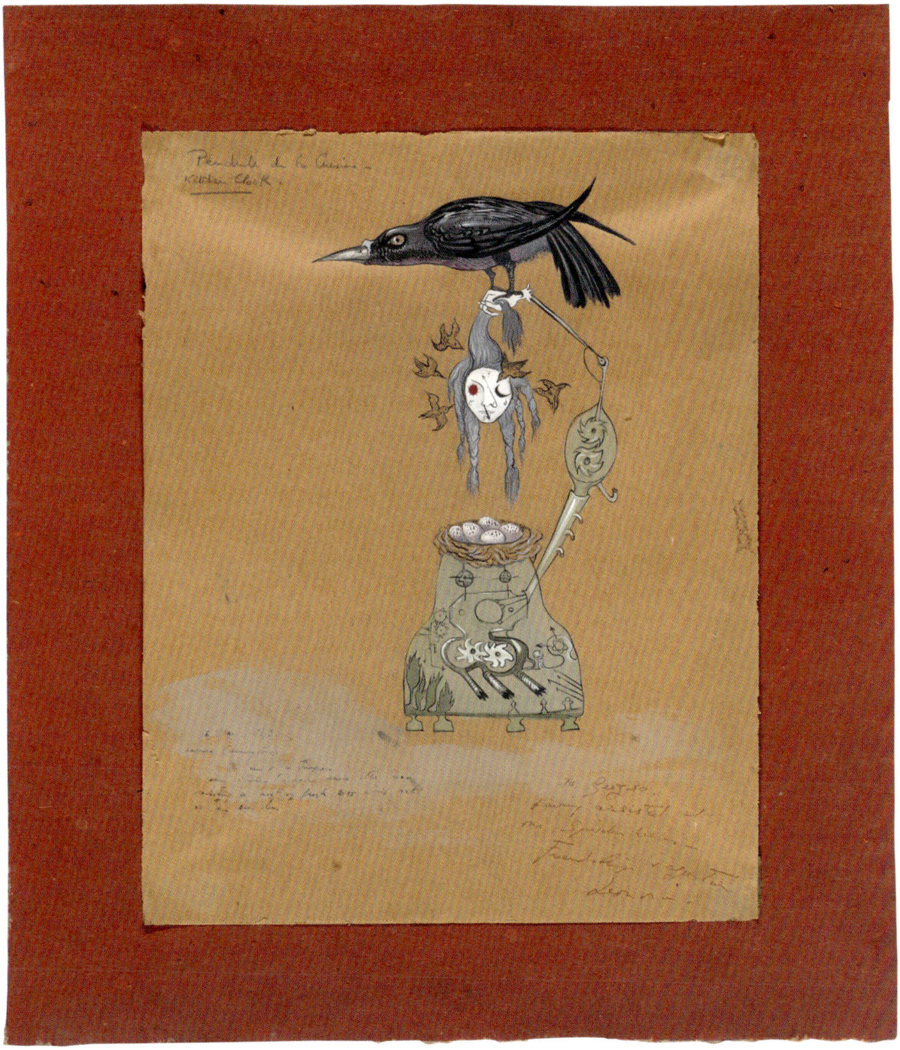

FIG. 31. Leonora Carrington (British, 1917–2011). *Kitchen Clock (Pendule de la cuisine)*. 1943. Watercolor, gouache, and pencil on colored paper, 16 ½ x 13 ⅞" (41.9 x 35.2 cm). THE MUSEUM OF MODERN ART, NEW YORK. COMMITTEE ON DRAWINGS AND PRINTS FUND

populated with women [**FIG. 30**]. The British artist Leonora Carrington also settled in Mexico after escaping war-torn Europe. In paintings and collages she built on Surrealist techniques while also elaborating a highly personal symbolism [**FIG. 31**]. Long ignored in favor of their more famous male colleagues, these and other women artists in Mexico during and after the war have become the focus of new research on their work and attention paid to their varied strategies for maintaining and asserting creative autonomy. For Kahlo, ironically enough, the key to developing a unique artistic persona was to explore the mutability of selfhood—with sincerity she scrutinized her personality and emotional life, and she laid bare the ways in which our sense of personal identity shifts according to the dictates of private and social experiences.

Although her work and image are nearly ubiquitous today, Kahlo's reputation languished for decades after her death, in 1954. It was only in the 1970s, when the question of why women artists had so long been ignored by the canon became urgent, that Kahlo was recognized as a pioneer in the picturing of female experience. Feminist artists in the United States such Judy Chicago and Miriam Schapiro incorporated references to her into their works, and the Chicano art movement embraced her as an uncompromising proponent of Mexican culture. In the twenty-first century Kahlo has remained a touchstone for artists questioning the stability of gender distinctions and the concepts of racial difference **[FIG. 32]**. In its intrepid dismantling of the notion of essential identity, *Self-Portrait with Cropped Hair* continues to raise questions about the intersection of our private experiences with the expectations of a broader social realm.

FIG. 32. Yasumasa Morimura (Japanese, born 1951). *An Inner Dialogue with Frida Kahlo (Self-Portrait with Cropped Hair 1)*. 2001. Color photograph, 59 x 44 ½" (150 x 113 cm). COURTESY THE ARTIST AND LUHRING AUGUSTINE, NEW YORK

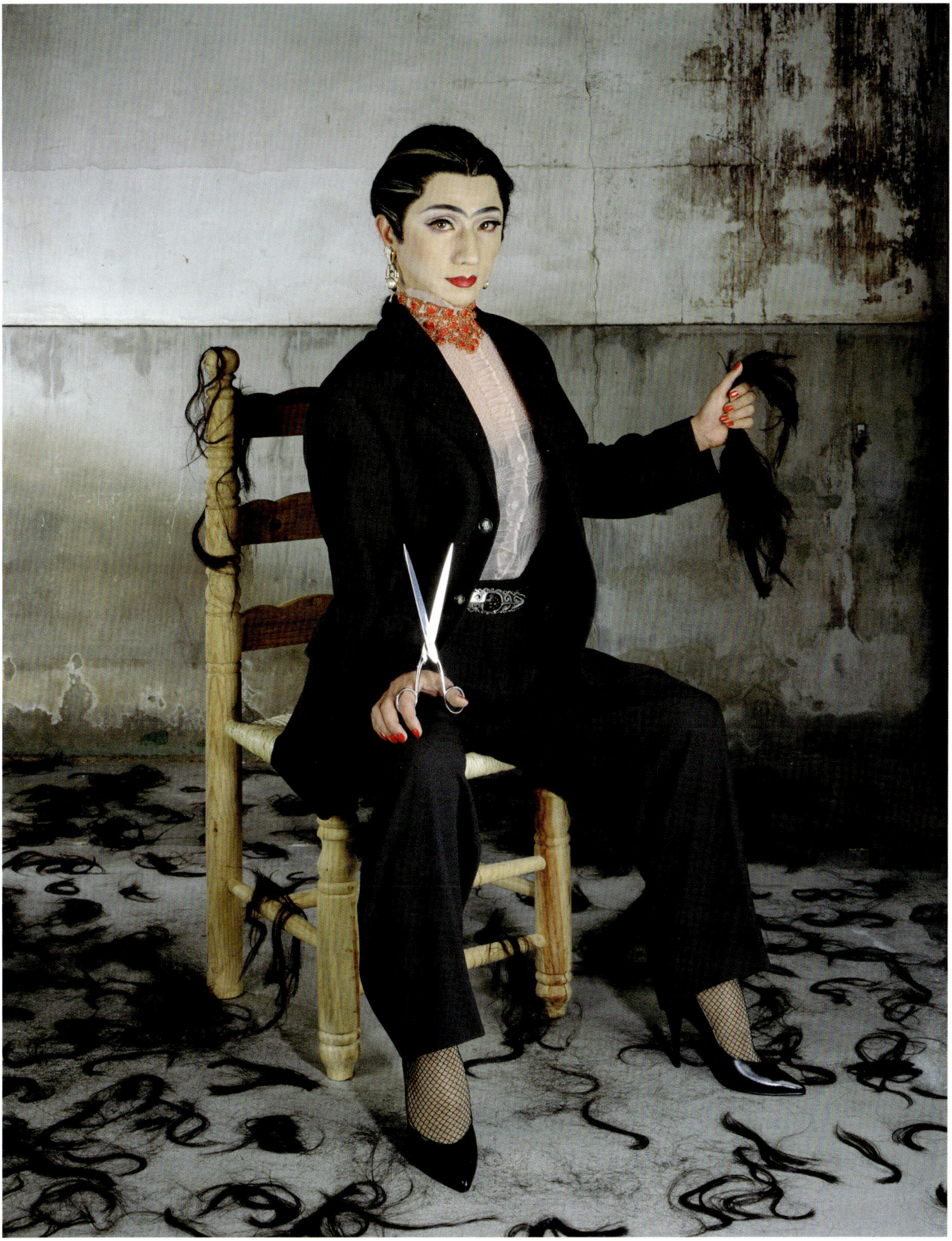

NOTES

1. Frida Kahlo, statement in Guggenheim grant application, 1940; quoted in in Sarah M. Lowe, *Frida Kahlo* (New York: Universe, 1991), p. 64.
2. Diego Rivera, "Frida Kahlo y el arte mexicana," *Boletin del Seminario de Cultura Mexicana* 1, no. 2 (October 1943); reprinted in English as "Frida Kahlo and Mexican Art," in Mark Francis, ed., *Frida Kahlo and Tina Modotti* (London: Whitechapel Art Gallery, 1982), p. 37.
3. This essay depends heavily on the scholarship of several key art historians. Hayden Herrera's biography of Kahlo spurred a reevaluation of her work by numerous scholars and has been a central source for the details on her life. See *Frida: A Biography of Frida Kahlo* (New York: Harper & Row, 1983). Lowe, Gannit Ankori, and Margaret A. Lindauer have elaborated the context in which Kahlo worked and have unpacked her multivalent and ever-changing public image. See Lowe, *Frida Kahlo*; Ankori, *Frida Kahlo* (London: Reaktion Books, 2013); and Lindauer, *Devouring Frida: The Art History and Popular Celebrity of Frida Kahlo* (Hanover, N.H.: University Press of New England, 1999).
4. Kahlo was so adamant about the importance of the Mexican Revolution to her development that she habitually claimed to have been born in 1910, the year the war started, rather than 1907, the year on her birth certificate. Lowe, *Frida Kahlo*, p. 13.
5. Laura Mulvey and Peter Wollen, "Frida Kahlo and Tina Modotti," in Francis, ed., *Frida Kahlo and Tina Modotti*, p. 18.
6. Herrera, *Frida Kahlo: The Paintings* (New York: Perennial, 2002), p. 48.
7. Lindauer, *Devouring Frida*, p. 107.
8. Herrera, *Frida*, p. 285.
9. Lindauer, *Devouring Frida*, pp. 44–45
10. Lowe, *Frida Kahlo*, p. 25.
11. Lindauer, *Devouring Frida*, p. 42.
12. André Breton, "Souvenir du Mexique," *Minotaure*, nos. 12–13 (May 1939): 40; quoted in English in Ilene Susan Fort and Tere Arcq, introduction to Fort and Arcq, eds. *In Wonderland: The Surrealist Adventures of Women Artists in Mexico and the United States* (Los Angeles: Los Angeles County Museum of Art, 2012), p. 22.
13. André Breton, "Frida Kahlo de Rivera," 1938, reprinted in English in *Surrealism and Painting*, trans. Simon Watson Taylor (London: Macdonald, 1972); and in Francis, ed., *Frida Kahlo and Tina Modotti*, p. 36.
14. Breton, "Frida Kahlo de Rivera," in Francis, ed., *Frida Kahlo and Tina Modotti*, p. 35; Julien Levy, in Herrera, *Frida*, p. 235.
15. "Art: Bomb Beribboned," *Time*, November 14, 1938, p. 29; quoted in Herrera, *Frida*, p. 231.
16. Bertram D. Wolfe, in Alyce Mahon, "The Lost Secret: Frida Kahlo and the Surrealist Imaginary," *Journal of Surrealism and the Americas* 5, nos. 1–2 (2011): 33.
17. The Julien Levy Gallery press release is reproduced in full in Herrera, *Frida*, p. 230.
18. Kahlo, in Antonio Rodríguez, "Frida Kahlo, expresionista de su yo interno," *Mañana*, n.d.; quoted in Herrera, *Frida*, p. 255.
19. Whitney Chadwick, *Women Artists and the Surrealist Movement* (New York: Thames and Hudson, 1985), pp. 7–12.
20. Breton, "Frida Kahlo de Rivera," in Francis, ed. *Frida Kahlo and Tina Modotti*, p. 36.

The Museum is deeply grateful to Fernando, Nadine, Ali, and Anisa Estrada-Karachi for making this publication possible.

FOR FURTHER READING

Ankori, Gannit. *Frida Kahlo*. London: Reaktion Books, 2013.

Carpenter, Elizabeth, ed. Frida Kahlo. Minneapolis: Walker Art Center, 2007.

Dexter, Emma, and Tanya Barson, eds. *Frida Kahlo*. London: Tate Publishing, 2005.

Fuentes, Carlos, et al. *Frida Kahlo: 1907–2007*. Mexico City: Instituto Nacional de Bellas Artes/Editorial RM; New York: D.A.P., 2000.

Herrera, Hayden. *Frida: A Biography of Frida Kahlo.* New York: Harper & Row, 1983.

Kahlo, Frida. *Escrituras*. Edited by Raquel Tibol. Mexico City: Universidad Nacional Autónoma de México, 1999.

Lindauer, Margaret A. *Devouring Frida: The Art History and Popular Celebrity of Frida Kahlo*. Hanover, N.H.: University Press of New England, 1999.

Lowe, Sarah. *Frida Kahlo*. New York: Universe, 1991.

Mulvey, Laura and Peter Wollen. *Frida Kahlo and Tina Modotti.* London: Whitechapel Art Gallery, 1982.

Produced by the Department of Publications, The Museum of Modern Art, New York

This publication is made possible by Fernando, Nadine, Ali, and Anisa Estrada-Karachi.

Edited by Emily Hall
Designed by Miko McGinty and Rita Jules
Production by Matthew Pimm
Printed and bound by Ofset Yapimevi, Turkey
This book is typeset in Ideal Sans. The paper is 150 gsm Magno Satin.

Library of Congress Control Number: 2018968465
ISBN: 978-1-63345-075-2

Published by The Museum of Modern Art
11 West 53 Street
New York, New York 10019-5497
www.moma.org

Distributed in the United States and Canada by Artbook | D.A.P.
75 Broad Street, Suite 630
New York, New York 10004
www.artbook.com

Distributed outside the United States and Canada by Thames & Hudson Ltd
181A High Holborn
London WC1V 7QX
www.thamesandhudson.com

Cover: Frida Kahlo. *Self-Portrait with Cropped Hair*. 1940. Oil on canvas, 15 ¾ x 11" (40 x 27.9 cm).
THE MUSEUM OF MODERN ART, NEW YORK. GIFT OF EDGAR KAUFMANN, JR.

Printed and bound in Turkey

PHOTOGRAPH CREDITS

In reproducing the images contained in this publication, the Museum obtained the permission of the rights holders whenever possible. If the Museum could not locate the rights holders, notwithstanding good-faith efforts, it requests that any contact information concerning such rights holders be forwarded so that they may be contacted for future editions.

All works by Frida Kahlo and Diego Rivera © 2019 Banco de México Diego Rivera Frida Kahlo Museums Trust, Mexico, D.F. / Artists Rights Society (ARS), New York

Alamy Stock Photo: figs. 2, 21, 24. The Art Institute of Chicago: fig. 9. Association Atelier André Breton / © 2019 Artists Rights Society (ARS), New York / ADAGP, Paris: fig. 25. Photograph © Christie's Images/Bridgeman Images: figs. 10, 15. Colección Andrés Blaisten, Mexico: figs. 6, 29. © 2019 The Jean Charlot Estate LLC / Member, Artists Rights Society (ARS), NY. Photograph © The Metropolitan Museum of Art / Art Resource, NY: fig. 5. © CNAC/MNAM/Dist. RMN-Grand Palais / Art Resource, NY: fig. 20. © 2019 Salvador Dalí, Fundació Gala-Salvador Dalí. Artists Rights Society / © CNAC/MNAM/ Dist. RMN-Grand Palais / Art Resource, NY: fig. 26. El Paso Museum of Art: fig. 11. Photograph © The Israel Museum, Jerusalem by Avshalom Avital / © 2019 Artists Rights Society (ARS), New York / VEGAP, Madrid: fig. 29. Museo Dolores Olmedo: figs. 13, 22. Department of Imaging Services, The Museum of Modern Art, New York: figs. 3, 7, 16; photograph by Kate Keller: covers, page 3, figs. 18, 27; photograph by Paige Knight: fig. 4. © 2019 Artists Rights Society (ARS), New York / Pro Litteris, Zurich: fig. 28. © 2019 Estate of Leonora Carrington / Artists Rights Society (ARS), New York: fig. 31. Harry Ransom Center, The University of Texas at Austin: fig. 1. The San Francisco Museum of Modern Art. Photograph by Ben Blackwell: fig. 12; photograph by Don Ross: fig. 17. Schalkwijk / Art Resource, NY: fig. 8. Courtesy Walker Art Center: fig. 14. The Vicente Wolfe Collection: fig. 19. © Yasumasa Morimura. Courtesy the artist and Luhring Augustine, New York: fig. 32.